P9-DMV-470

GERMANY'S PANZER ARM
IN WWII

0 11557 03342 7

Other titles in the Stackpole Military History Series

THE AMERICAN CIVIL WAR

Cavalry Raids of the Civil War
Pickett's Charge
Witness to Gettysburg

WORLD WAR II

Armor Battles of the Waffen-SS, 1943–45
Australian Commandos
The B-24 in China
Beyond the Beachhead
The Brandenburger Commandos
Bringing the Thunder
Coast Watching in World War II
Fist from the Sky
Flying American Combat Aircraft of World War II
Forging the Thunderbolt
Grenadiers
Infantry Aces
Luftwaffe Aces
Messerschmitts over Sicily
Michael Wittmann and the Waffen SS Tiger Commanders
of the Leibstandarte in World War II, Volume One
Michael Wittmann and the Waffen SS Tiger Commanders
of the Leibstandarte in World War II, Volume Two
On the Canal
Packs On!
Panzer Aces
Panzer Aces II
Surviving Bataan and Beyond
The 12th SS, Volume One
The 12th SS, Volume Two
Tigers in the Mud

THE COLD WAR / VIETNAM

Flying American Combat Aircraft: The Cold War
Land with No Sun
Street without Joy

WARS OF THE MIDDLE EAST

Never-Ending Conflict

GERMANY'S PANZER ARM
IN WWII

R. L. DiNardo

STACKPOLE
BOOKS

Copyright © 1997 by R. L. DiNardo

Published in paperback in 2006 by
STACKPOLE BOOKS
5067 Ritter Road
Mechanicsburg, PA 17055
www.stackpolebooks.com

Originally published as GERMANY'S PANZER ARM, by R. L. DiNardo, in
hard cover by Praeger, an imprint of Greenwood Publishing Group, Inc.,
Westport, CT. Copyright © 1997 by R. L. DiNardo. Paperback edition by
arrangement with Greenwood Publishing Group, Inc. All rights reserved.

All photos courtesy of Christian Ankerstjerne

Printed in the United States of America

10 9 8 7 6 5 4 3 2 1

FIRST EDITION

Library of Congress Cataloging-in-Publication Data

DiNardo, R. L.
  [Gemany's panzer arm]
  Germany's panzer arm in World War II / R.L. DiNardo.
  p. cm. — (Stackpole Military history series)
  Originally published: Germany's panzer arm. Praeger : Westport, CT,
c1997. (Contributions in military studies, 0883-6884 ; no. 166)
  Includes bibliographical references and index.
  ISBN-13: 978-0-8117-3342-7
  ISBN-10: 0-8117-3342-4
  1. Germany. Heer—Armored troops—History. 2. Germany. Heer—
Organization. 3. Military doctrine—Germany—History—20th century.
I. Title. II. Series.

UA714.D55 2006
358'.180943—dc22
                                                        2006011556

Table of Contents

Photographs follow page 70

Acknowledgments

People relatively unfamiliar with the process of researching and writing a book might regard it as being rather laborious. To some degree this is true, but it can be wonderful at the same time. This is largely because of the delightful people one meets along the way. At the National Archives, Drs. George Wagner, Harry Rilley and Robin Cookson always provided excellent assistance to me in my research trips to Washington, D.C. I am indebted to Colonel Steve Bowman, Dr. Richard Sommers, Louise Arnold-Friend and the rest of the staff at the United States Army Military History Institute at Carlisle, Pa., for their aid and assistance in my frequent trips there.

Since most of this book was completed during my tenure as Visiting Professor at the Air War College at Maxwell AFB, Alabama, I must acknowledge the help and support of some of my colleagues. James Corum, of the School of Advanced Airpower Studies, was kind enough to lend me some of his considerable files, especially the Wolfram von Richthofen papers, and was always a fountain of interesting observations on the German Army, especially on our frequent shotgun shooting excursions. My department chairmen, Colonel Bryant Shaw and Prof. Alexander S. Cochran, were always generous with financial support for several research trips to Washington, D.C. I also want to thank Cols. Ray Bean, Dave Roll, Dale Autry, Robyn Read and Stef Eisen for their support, as well as Profs. James Mowbray, Grant Hammond, Judith Gentleman and Sharyl Cross. Most of all, I am grateful to my friend and colleague, Prof. Daniel J. Hughes. Dan was always generous with his time, his massive library on the German

Army, and his growing collection of microfilm rolls of captured German documents copied from the National Archives.

Since this book began as a dissertation I would be remiss if I did not acknowledge and thank my fellow graduate students and friends for their support: Sheila Rabin, Irving Kelter, Janice Gordon-Kelter, Carl Slater, Albert Nofi, Jay Stone, Kathy Williams, Valerie Eads, Andrea Martin, Robert Croker, Ron and Peggy Furqueron and Martin McDowell. Most of all, I would like to thank Maria Boes. Her patience and hard work was instrumental in enabling me to master the intricacies and mysteries of the German language. Special thanks to my dear friends Scott Rosenthal and Mary Hansen, for their support and generous hospitality every time I go to Washington. Most of all, I would like to thank my family for having the patience to put up with me through all this.

A dissertation represents much more than the simple completion of a research project. It is the culmination of an extended period of education. I want to thank my undergraduate professors for providing an excellent education, especially Cynthia Whittaker. My dissertation supervisor, David Syrett, always provided wise counsel and direction in the course of this project. Professor Patrick Abbazia served as my third reader, and also provided sage advice between extended conversations about our common passion, the New York Giants. Both of these men exemplify what graduate professors should be to their students. Finally, there was my second reader, Professor William O. Shanahan. "Wild Bill," as he was affectionately known by those of us who had the privilege of studying with him, was truly a "generalist" in the very best sense of the word. His wide range of interests, and the joy he brought to the graduate school seminar room were always a wonder to behold. He greatly influenced many of us at the Graduate Center of CUNY in so many positive ways. Professor Shanahan was retired but stayed on to serve as second reader when this dissertation was successfully defended in 1988. He passed away in 1990, well before this book was brought to completion. It is dedicated to his memory.

Although a great many people have been mentioned here, all of the work presented in this book is mine and mine alone. I alone am responsible for all errors of commission or omission.

Introduction

"While the rise of Hitler changed the map of
Europe more quickly than even Napoleon had
done—though for a shorter period—it was the rise
of the armored forces in the German Army that
mainly enabled him to achieve his run of con-
quests. Without them his dreams would never have
turned into realities."

—B. H. LIDDELL-HART[1]

No twentieth-century military machine has generated a
larger corpus of literature than the German Army of
World War II. A vast number of studies have been published
dealing with the activities of the General Staff and its relationship with Adolf Hitler. There have also been numerous
studies of the various campaigns, and a few of the various
branches of the Army, with major attention being devoted to
the panzer arm.[2]

For many people with an interest in World War II, the
"darling," if such a term might ever be used in this context, of
the war was the German panzer force. It was led by some of
Germany's most dashing field commanders such as Heinz
Guderian, Erwin Rommel and Hasso von Manteuffel, to name
a few. It has certainly drawn the lion's share of publications
dealing with specific elements of the Army.

Yet, this body of literature in regards to the panzer arm is
incomplete. Many books on it are often of a technical nature
and are little concerned with other matters. Many other books
are of the "picture book" type favored by model or regalia

buffs, with titles such as SS Serbo-Croatian Panzers in Action, to tickle their interest. Memoirs abound, but these too are often unsatisfying. Many, with Erich von Manstein being a prime example, are written by former generals in tones that can be described as irritatingly pompous, glorifying their own self-professed brilliance, and are all too often of little use. Others, Heinz Guderian in particular, ascribe the success of the panzer arm to the simple implementation of the ideas of the British thinkers J.F.C. Fuller and B. H. Liddell-Hart, for reasons having more to do with the post-war situation in Europe than with historical truth.[3] In short, there are almost no really integrated studies of the armor branch dealing with those organizational, economic, personnel, doctrinal and tactical factors that affected the panzer arm's performance, and how they are related to each other. It is precisely this gap which this study will attempt to fill.

Of all the considerations mentioned above, organization is perhaps the most underrated. How an army and its sub-units are organized can often confer an advantage that can affect the outcome of a campaign. A fine example of this would be Napoleon's campaigns of 1805 and 1806, where his corps d'armee system gave him a significant advantage over his Austrian, Russian and Prussian enemies, whose armies were organized along more traditional eighteenth century lines.

Since the standard German panzer unit was the panzer division, this study will examine its organization from 1933 and 1945. During this period the German panzer division went through a plethora of reorganizations, the most important of which was carried out in the autumn of 1940. The higher organizations into which the panzer divisions were integrated will also be analyzed. The purpose of chapter five is to analyze the positive and negative aspects of German organization and how these affected operational performance in the field. Also to be examined are those factors that influenced German divisional organization and the performance of the panzer arm in operations. These would include equipment, personnel policies, training and doctrine.

Chapter one on equipment will naturally cover primarily armored fighting vehicles and equipment used by the Germans. This chapter, however, must also address several important questions about the general nature of both the German Army and the German economy. Always bear in mind that the panzer arm, while the most modern element of the Germany Army, constituted a relatively small portion of it. The vast majority of the Army consisted of marching infantry, which relied largely on horses for transport.[4] Given this, the following questions must be asked. What was the true nature of Germany's rearmament? How did this affect the development of the panzer arm? Did Germany possess the economic base needed for the creation and maintenance of a large armored force? Could the German Army have been more modern than it was? Should Germany, given its continental priorities, have devoted scarce resources to the construction of a navy? The answers to these questions will allow for a broad evaluation of German equipment, as well as observations about how well or poorly the German economy operated both before and during the war. Also relevant in this area are such issues as the tank versus assault gun question and the German propensity for building many different models of the same vehicle.

The personnel who fill a division's organization and do the actual fighting are, of course, the most important element of any military establishment. Chapter two of this study will include a general survey of how personnel were selected for panzer units, including those panzer units raised by the Luftwaffe and the SS. This chapter will examine a number of issues vital to an understanding of the German Army. The first of these is the German conscription system and the internecine warfare waged by the three services for their respective shares of the available manpower. Within this issue the conflict between the Army and the SS also comes into focus, as well as the territorial system employed by the Germans for the purposes of conscription. Some attention will also be focused on the Anschluss, and the question of how the German Army was able to absorb the Austrian Army.

Tactical superiority has always been one of the keystones of German military prowess. Yet how much of this was due to pre-combat training or to simple improvization in the field? This question is best dealt with in chapter three by examining German manuals and unit training orders and then comparing them to operations in the field.

For doctrine, the question is slightly different. Here it must be asked, how much of the German Army's armor doctrine was indigenous, and how much of it was derived from foreign theorists? This question has always brought forth strong opinions from historians on both sides of the issues. Dealing with these questions will allow for a full evaluation of the importance of General Heinz Guderian's writings and the influence of the more famous British theorists, especially B. H. Liddell-Hart and J.F.C. Fuller.

This study hopes to provide some insights into the rise and decline of the most important part of the German Army. To be sure, this will not be a "battle book." Although campaigns and battles will be alluded to, none will be covered in detail. Rather, this study will concentrate on some of the nuts and bolts aspects of the German Army's expansion and its absorption of two foreign armies. It will also provide a rigorous examination of German doctrine. Hopefully, this study will not only be a complete study of the German panzer arm, but also provide a microcosmic view of Nazi Germany at war, as well as some insights into the nature of the German Army.

CHAPTER ONE

Equipment and Economy

"That's what I need! That's what I want to have."
—ADOLF HITLER, 1933[1]

"The German Army must be operational in four years. The German economy must be capable of supporting war in four years."
—ADOLF HITLER, 1936[2]

"The preservation and strengthening of the German panzer arm is all the more vital at present, as our enemies' annual production of about 50,000 tanks weighs heavily against us . . ."
—HEINZ GUDERIAN, 1943[3]

"Hitler's generals, raised on the dogma of Clausewitz and Moltke, could not understand that war is won in the factories."
—JOSEPH STALIN, 1949[4]

An armored or motorized force is heavily dependent on the quality and quantity of its equipment, and the German panzer force was no exception to this. In considering the question of the panzer arm's equipment, however, to simply look at the technical specifications of tanks and their performance in combat would be woefully inadequate. A number of other aspects must be explored. First, the nature of the German economy and its ability to produce the requisite equipment, especially motor vehicles, must be dealt with. The techniques used in the production of vehicles must also be considered, as well as obtaining the requisite amount of oil needed to fuel them. Another factor to be considered in Germany's rearmament is the ability of the German economy to support the equipping of three services. Finally, disruption in the economy, both internal and external, must be considered, as well as combat losses and their effects on the fighting ability of German armored units.

For a country to equip and maintain a large armored or motorized force in the field, several prerequisites must be achieved. Since these units rely primarily on motor vehicles, a country must have a well-developed motor vehicle industry to provide the necessary number of vehicles. An obvious corollary to this is a substantial oil refining industry, or at least a guaranteed supply of oil, without which the vehicles are useless. Another important element is an efficient maintenance service for the repair of damaged or broken down vehicles. Combat vehicles also require several kinds of highly sophisticated equipment, such as electrical wiring, radio communications, and high-quality optics.

According to B.H. Liddell-Hart, there are some twenty basic raw materials vital to the waging of modern war: coal, wood, iron, rubber, oil, copper, nickel, lead, glycerine, cellulose, mercury, platinum, antimony, manganese, asbestos, mica, nitric acid and sulphur.[5] Germany was lacking in almost all of these. For our purposes, however, we shall concentrate on the three materials vital to the production of tanks and motor vehicles, namely steel, oil and rubber.

Right from the start, Germany's position in steel production was precarious. Germany was one of the major steel producers in Europe, but lacked an indigenous supply of high grade iron ore. Germany did have a sizeable amount of low grade iron ore, and Hitler did call for German steel producers to increase the amount of German ore extracted. German steel producers balked at this, however, as they considered the extraction of low grade German ore both impractical and too expensive.[6]

As part of the ideological goal of achieving autarky (a form of economic self-sufficiency), Hitler set up the Four Year Plan under Reichsmarschall Hermann Göring in 1936. Part of Göring's charter was to increase the extraction of German iron ore, thus making Germany less dependent on the importation of foreign ore.[7] Although Göring's organization did make strenuous efforts to increase the use of German iron ore, it proved insufficient to meet Germany's need for weapons grade steel. During the pre-war period, Germany received most of its iron ore from Sweden, Germany imported annually about 71% of Sweden's total iron ore production.[8] This dependence continued during the war, and reached a high point in 1943 when Germany imported 10.3 million tons of iron ore from Sweden.[9] During the pre-war period, Germany also imported fairly substantial amounts of iron ore from the Soviet Union and the countries of southeastern Europe.[10] Given circumstances such as these, Germany entered the period of rearmament, and later the war, poorly prepared.

Germany's position with regard to oil was very weak as well. In 1933 Germany produced 233,000 tons of crude oil.[11] This was insignificant compared with Romania's production of 7,377,000 tons and the Soviet Union's output of 21,489,000 tons.[12] Matters were not improved by Hitler's contradictory desires in this area. Being a convinced autarkist, he wanted Germany to become self-sufficient in oil and become a fully motorized economy, but projects such as the *autobahnen* and the production of the *volkswagen* only served to increase oil consumption. Although German crude oil production increased by about 90% between 1933 and 1936, it proved insufficient to meet the demands created by Germany's 56% increase in oil consumption during the same period.[13]

Given these circumstances, Germany had to depend on imports. In 1934, for example, Germany consumed about 3,000,000 tons of petroleum products, of which 85% were imported.[14] The Austrian *Anschluss*, while giving Germany an additional source of iron ore, did little to improve the situation.[15] Given the importance of oil, Hitler did try to create a strategic reserve of oil. On 24 August 1934 the government set up an organization called the *Wirtschaftliche Forschungsge-*

sellschaft (*Wifo*). Part of its mandate was to create a strategic reserve of certain raw materials, including oil.[16] Just after his appointment as Chancellor, Hitler endorsed a plan to import and refine American oil, which would then be stockpiled in the strategic reserve. Presumably, this effort was subsumed into *Wifo*'s charter. Nothing, however, came of the idea.[17]

If Germany did have one advantage, it was in its ability to produce synthetic oil. The first synthetic oil plant was built in Germany after World War I. The synthetic oil program was supported by the military, but the only company to express interest in this rather expensive process was I. G. Farben. The depression almost destroyed the synthetic program when it created an oil glut, but its survival and expansion were ensured by Hitler's coming to power.[18] Although ahead of the rest of the world in this area, Germany's synthetic oil program in 1938 amounted to only about 1,600,000 tons.[19]

Rubber was another raw material that was very scarce in Germany. With Germany solely dependent on imported rubber, Hitler sought to remedy this situation. Part of the charter of Göring's Four Year Plan was to increase the production of synthetic rubber.[20] Despite these efforts, Germany's rubber situation would remain difficult throughout the war.

Germany's ability to produce the requisite equipment for the panzer arm was limited by several other factors, the prime factor being the question of who was responsible for the direction of the process of rearmament, not to mention the economy as a whole. Hitler himself never issued a directive which could be taken as a general plan for the course of Germany's military expansion.[21] Initially, the authority for rearmament rested with two agencies. The first was the Wehrmacht's Office of Economics and Armaments (*Wirtschafts and Rüstungs Amt*, or *Wi Rü Amt*), successor to the Army's Economics Staff which had been created in 1924.[22] The other was the Reich Ministry of Economics (*Reichswirtschaftsministerium*, or RWM), headed by Dr. Hjalmar Schacht.

Then in 1936, ostensibly for the purpose of making Germany ready for war, Hitler created the "Four Year Plan," and placed the agency under Hermann Göring. This was a poor decision in two ways. First, although Hitler chose Göring for his "energy," the Reichsmarschall knew nothing about economics and openly said so.[23] The choice of Göring also did not bode well for the Army and Navy, as he was both Minister of Aviation and Commander of the Luftwaffe, and could thus be expected to starve the other two services of resources in favor of his own. Hitler further complicated this unhealthy situation in 1940 by creating the Ministry of Armaments and Munitions under Dr. Fritz Todt. In February 1942 Albert Speer succeeded Todt when the latter was killed in a plane crash.

The structure of the economy had several unfortunate effects, the prime of which was the question of who actually ran the economy. Hitler, as noted previously, did not take an active role in the overall direction of the economy and rearmament in the pre-war period. Göring stated after the war that he and Schacht encountered jurisdictional problems almost immediately after his appointment.[24] There was also an ideological component to the conflict between Göring and Schacht. Göring was a confirmed autarkist, while Schacht saw autarky as being contrary to the basic principles of civilization.[25] The creation and expansion of the *Reichswerke Hermann Göring*, however, made Schacht's eclipse a certainty, and Schacht resigned in early 1938.

The Armed Forces High Command (*Oberkommando der Wehrmacht*, or OKW) also had concerns about Göring's appointment. Their economic staff (later *Wi Rü Amt*) strenuously opposed Göring's appointment.[26] Even worse, there was not even a strong regulating mechanism among the armed services themselves. Ideally *Wi Rü Amt* was supposed to coordinate the armament programs of the three services and the head of *Wi Rü Amt*, General Georg Thomas, did issue guidelines and directives to this end. None of the services, however, abided by them.[27] Thus the services competed not only against the civilian economy, but against each other as well. Although Speer succeeded in imposing order on this chaos in 1943, it was far too late to affect the war's outcome.

Another factor detrimental to Germany's armament effort was the continued priority of the civilian sector of the economy. As late as 1938, civilian construction projects still had high priority. These included buildings to stage future Nazi party congresses and the *autobahnen*.[28] In 1943, for example, Germany produced some 120,000 typewriters, 13,000 duplicating machines, 50,000 address machines, 3,000 accounting machines, 200,000 radios, 150,000 electric bedwarmers and 3,600 refrigerators.[29] Although harmful militarily, this did give Germany a degree of political stability that was absent in World War I.[30]

The amount of slack in the German economy has been the subject of a great deal of historical study that has yielded very different interpretations. Alan Milward saw it as a system that allowed maximum flexibility and the shifting of priorities.[31] More recent scholarship has portrayed the process of German rearmament as either complete chaos or an attempt at total mobilization that was simply grossly mismanaged.[32] Perhaps the best explanation has been provided by Richard Overy, who has argued that ultimately the German economy "fell between two stools," reflecting some aspects of both the Soviet and American economies, but unable to imitate the achievements of either.[33] In any case, the structure and organization of the German economy was not well-suited to satisfy the demands of a large armored force.

The degree of motorization in the German Army in general and the size of the armored force was affected in a broad way by German military policy. This matter could best be expressed in a question: should Germany have built a sizeable surface navy? That large resources were devoted to the construction of ships such as the *Bismarck, Tirpitz,* and *Graf Zeppelin* was a bit surprising, given Hitler's initial thinking on the subject. In his second book, Hitler wrote that the High Seas Fleet contributed nothing to Germany's war effort in World War I:

The land army was really the German weapon grown out of a hundred-year tradition, but in the end our fleet was only a romantic plaything, a parade piece that was built for its own sake and which again for its own sake could not be risked. The whole benefit which it brought us is disproportionate to the terrible enmity with which it saddled us.[34]

This kind of thinking was certainly consonant with German strategic thinking during the late Weimar period. Defense Minister Wilhelm Groener felt that the Navy's role should be confined to protecting Germany's sea lanes in the Baltic, and these inclinations were certainly shared by Hitler, at least initially, as well as by Groener's successor as Defense Minister, Field Marshal Werner von Blomberg.[35]

The Navy High Command, however, had very different views. Grand Admiral Erich Raeder, Commander of the Germany Navy, did not want the Navy's operations essentially confined to the Baltic. Raeder, accurately described by Wilhelm Deist as a "Tirpitzian," regarded the Atlantic as the proper focus for German naval operations, and sought to develop a fleet capable of carrying out such a task.[36] Raeder met Hitler for the first time in the spring of 1933, and was able to convince him of the utility of a surface navy, especially as a political instrument. In addition, Raeder proved very skillful at bureaucratic infighting with the other two services.[37]

The Navy was also aided by a shift in Hitler's thinking from his original position about a large navy as reflected in the quotation cited above, which was written sometime in 1928.[38] After the resolution of the Munich crisis, Hitler began to anticipate the need to deal definitively with the western powers, especially Britain and the United States. This would require a large navy as well as an expanded Luftwaffe. Therefore, after Munich the Navy became the chief recipient of Germany's armament efforts, while the Luftwaffe developed the Ju-88 as its new bomber.[39]

The trouble was that once Hitler gave his blessing to large-scale naval construction, the Navy proceeded to engage in a building program that was completely unrelated to those of the other services. Naval expansion was essentially based on Raeder's rather wishful thinking on the German Navy's place among the major naval powers. This was ultimately expressed in the wildly ambitious "Z Plan," which called for a navy of 365 ships, including six battleships and four aircraft carriers by 1944.[40]

From the point of view of the German Army and the panzer arm, the decision to build a navy was one of Hitler's worst. To be sure there were some who felt early on that the resources being committed to naval construction were being wasted. One author argued that scrapping one "pocket battle-ship" would save a great deal of raw material and oil which could instead be devoted to the production of tanks and motor vehicles.[41] There was a good deal of truth to this, as the Navy's expansion was utterly unrealistic, not to mention waste-ful. In November 1937, for example, the Navy was allocated 74,000 tons of steel, but could not use all of it. A Navy esti-mate of mobilization requirements for the Z Plan dated 31 December 1938 called for 6,000,000 tons of oil, plus 2,000,000 tons of diesel fuel. This was higher than the total German oil consumption for 1938, and three times higher than German oil production for the year.[42] Thus for the panzer arm, the expansion of the German Navy was a gross misuse of scarce resources.

The panzer arm was also affected by the matter of who built the tanks it used. In war, one needs almost everything in large numbers, including men, guns, vehicles and, of course, tanks. Since tanks are required in large numbers, they are best produced by industries acquainted with the facets of mass pro-duction. As tanks are automotive devices, they are best pro-duced by automobile companies. This was certainly the case with the American Sherman tank, which was produced by the combined efforts of Ford, Chrysler, and General Motors.[43] This was not the case in Germany. To begin with, the German military was mistrustful of mass production. The material pro-duced by mass production was regarded as substandard and shoddy.[44] Also, in Germany the companies that produced tanks also produced railroad equipment, especially locomotives.[45] The techniques used in the construction of railroad equipment did not lend themselves to the techniques used in mass production. The situation was made worse by the fact that Germany suffered from a shortage of rolling stock, a problem which had to be addressed.[46] During much of the war, a great deal of resources had to be devoted to the production of rolling stock. During the critical years of the war, 1941–1943, Germany produced 9,798 locomotives and 172,000 pieces of rolling stock.[47] This was certainly an inhibiting factor in German tank production.

Another problem faced by the armor branch was that of constantly having to develop new tanks. Although Germany had been conducting experiments on the development of tanks throughout the 1920s and early 1930s, in 1939 Germany went to war with an armor force that had a large number of obsolete tanks.[48] In 1939, the vast majority of the Army's tank park consisted of either Pz Is or Pz IIs. Even before the French campaign General Franz Halder, the chief of the General Staff, rated the Pz I as being good only against a weak or demoralized enemy and the Pz II as being only slightly better.[49]

To upgrade the quality of the German armor force before the invasion of the Soviet Union, most of the Pz Is and some of the Pz IIs were removed from active service and replaced by the more modern Pz III and Pz IV, although the older machines were still kept in the total park. The result was that although Germany's total tank park increased in size over the period 1 April 1940 to 1 June 1941 from 3,387 to 5,694, some 2,034 tanks (36%) were obsolete models. To make matters worse, delivery of the newer Pz III and Pz IV lagged well behind the "planned" figures announced by Hitler and Todt.[50] It is also important to bear in mind that at this time, due to the divisional reorganization undertaken by the Army, the number of panzer divisions was effectively doubled. This spread the tank force even more thinly.

The Germans also hurt themselves by building a large number of variations of the same model. From 1934 to 1945

the Germans produced four versions of the Pz I, ten versions
of the Pz II, thirteen versions of the Pz III, ten versions of the
Pz IV, four versions of the Pz V (Panther), and several versions
of the Pz VI (Tiger).[51] There were also several variations of
the two models of captured Czech tanks used by the Germans,
the Pz 35 and the Pz 38.

The primary reason for this unhealthy state of affairs was a
profusion of overlapping authorities. The Army's Ordnance
Department had a committee for the development of any new
weapon. The Ministry of Armaments and Munitions also had
such committees, which had to deal with the designers and
producers of the weapons. Troops in the field also had input
into this process. During the periods between campaigns,
units conducted tests on vehicles. An example of this would
be the tests conducted by the 11th Panzer Regiment on the Pz
III and Pz IV from December 1939 to January 1940 to see how
they performed in winter conditions.[52] In some cases, upgunning or increasing the armor of existing tank models produced new sub-types, which led to an even greater profusion
of vehicle types. In any case, deficiencies were noted by the
troops, and would then be corrected in later versions of the
vehicle. Hitler also affected this process. Being fascinated by
technical devices and machines, he often personally ordered
design changes in armored vehicles.[53] The wasteful production of numerous versions of the same vehicle continued until
1944, when Speer was able to rationalize German production
down to a few models.[54] Once again, this was far too late to
affect the outcome of the war.

The profusion of vehicle types created several serious
problems. First, the introduction of new types always created
delays in production, because a certain amount of time was
always required for retooling. In addition, changes such as
putting in a heavier gun with a longer barrel or adding thicker
armor added weight to the vehicle, while the engine remained
the same. The Pz IV B, for example, armed with a short 75mm
gun, weighed about 19.5 tons when it was produced in 1938.
The Pz IV F2, which went into service in 1942, had a longer

75mm gun and thicker armor. These changes, however, increased the tank's weight to 26 tons, a 25% increase. Both vehicles, however, were powered by the Maybach HL 120 TRM engine.[55] The added weight put much greater strain on the engine, thus leading to increased wear and tear.

Even more important was the problem of field maintenance. In order to be effective, vehicles require a steady supply of spare parts. This was a requirement that German industry completely failed to meet. Burkhart Müller-Hillebrand blamed this situation on "some armament production officials."[56] Albert Speer took the more standard course of blaming Hitler.[57] Whatever the case, the German Army faced an almost continuous shortage of spare parts, a situation made even worse by the profusion of models, which made the distribution of those spare parts that were produced even more difficult. At times, Army Groups received spare parts for tank models that they did not even have.[58]

Another problem was the German automobile industry. A panzer division is not simply based on tanks alone. To be effective, a tank needs to be supported by a variety of vehicles, the most important of which are the trucks needed to tow artillery and carry gasoline, ammunition and men. Yet it is quite clear that Germany did not possess the automobile industry needed to fulfill the demands of Germany's panzer arm.

Albert Speer believed that Germany's automobile industry was working up to standards of modern efficiency when he took up his duties in February 1942.[59] In fact, however, the German automobile industry was poorly suited to meeting Germany's needs for fighting a modern war, and was underutilized in any case. There was apparently no system in place by 1939 for converting the automobile industry to war production and in fact, even as late as 1944, the Army was still using large numbers of civilian trucks, which were quite unsuited to military service.[60] Since the German motor vehicle industry was incapable of satisfying the German Army's needs, the German had to resort to the very risky expedient of using captured equipment.

By 1939 the Germans already had extensive experience in handling captured equipment in their occupations of Austria and Czechoslovakia. The Austrian material was easily incorporated into the German Army. A considerable amount of material was captured in Czechoslovakia, including 810 tanks.[61] This material, however, was poorly handled. Each of the divisions of the occupation force gathered equipment and shipped each piece to various ordnance offices in Germany. This was a serious mistake, as all of the writing on the equipment was in Czech, which few Germans could read.[62] The Germans were fortunate, however, in that both the *Anschluss* and the annexation of the Sudetenland were essentially peacetime operations, which allowed them the opportunity to profit from their mistakes. Nonetheless, the dependence on the use of captured vehicles in large numbers did not bode well for the future.

The outbreak of war quickly magnified all the deficiencies in Germany's panzer arm due to the inadequacies of the German economy. Although the victory over Poland was relatively cheap, problems arose almost immediately. Shortages of trucks were experienced throughout the Polish campaign.[63] Halder noted on 3 February 1940 that the Army was being allotted only 1,000 trucks per month, not even enough to replace normal wastage, let alone combat losses. This, however, represented slightly over 25% of the total German truck production of 3,979 for February 1940.[64] This led to the Chief of the General Staff to consider the demotorization of a number of infantry divisions.[65] Haider's comments on the weakness of German tanks has already been noted.

Even worse from Germany's standpoint was the raw material situation. Although Germany received fairly substantial amounts of iron ore from southeastern Europe Sweden, as noted earlier, remained Germany's main supplier of iron ore. This trade was eventually curtailed by Allied diplomatic pressure after 1943. Strenuous efforts were also made by the Royal Air Force to lay mines to stop coastal traffic. The Royal Navy also employed light forces at the Rhine estuary off Holland towards the same purpose.[66] For other materials the Germans resorted to some interesting improvisations. Germany was able to increase its stock of nickel by 50% when the government recalled all nickel coins in Germany for melting down in 1939.[67]

Oil was a far more serious problem. Romania remained Germany's main supplier of oil. In 1939 alone Germany imported some 1,272,000 tons of oil.[68] In addition to being Germany's main supplier of oil, Romania also provided Italy with about 2,000,000 tons of oil annually until July 1943.[69] It is also important to note that Romanian oil fields were vulnerable, at least initially, to Allied pressure, as they were largely owned by either French or British companies.[70] The Polish campaign did very little to improve this situation. According to the terms of the Nazi-Soviet Pact, the Soviets occupied about 70% of Poland's oil producing areas.[71] Hitler therefore considered it imperative that the industrially developed west be quickly conquered to alleviate Germany's raw material situation.[72] Regardless of those anticipated benefits, Hitler still sought to strengthen his ties with Romanian oil sources. On 27 May 1940, Germany signed the "Oil Pact" with Romania, by which Germany would trade arms for oil.[73]

The conquest of France and the Low Countries most certainly improved Germany's raw material position and was vital to the panzer force. To deal with the seizing and stockpiling of raw materials, *Wi Rü Amt* created the office of inspector for seizing and stockpiling of raw materials, covering Belgium and occupied France, under Major General Robert Buhrmann. After his death in October 1940, the post was occupied by a Luftwaffe officer, Major General Walter Wittring. Captain Hans Schu was made responsible for the collection of scrap and old metal, a task he had performed in Poland.[74] Through the efforts of these men, by the end of 1941, occupied France provided Germany with 107,841 tons of iron and steel, as well as 912,761 tons of scrap metal.[75] Although France did not produce a great deal of oil, all of France's oil installations were captured intact when attempts to demolish them miscarried.[76]

The Germans also captured an enormous quantity of equipment, of which extensive use was made. Here again the Germans profited greatly from the experience gained in the bloodless occupation of Czechoslovakia. For the French campaign, captured English and French vehicles were collected in special vehicle parks. In the case of the Fourth Army, the vehicle park for captured vehicles was located in La Chapelle-sur-Erde, almost five miles north of Nantes.[77] The facility was under the supervision of the 561st Army Vehicle Park. Any repairs that the captured vehicles needed would be done by French mechanics from Nantes.[78]

The number of French vehicles pressed into service by the Germans was vital to the expansion of the panzer and motorized infantry divisions, as well as the Army as a whole. According to one German officer, "French motor vehicles were indispensable to the invasion of Russia."[79] The 20th Panzer Division, as well as the 14th, 18th and 20th Motorized Infantry Divisions, were all equipped with French motor vehicles.[80] Although French tanks were not suitable for German style operations, the Germans gave them to shattered panzer formations rebuilding in France. This gave them the strength to undertake internal security missions in occupied France.[81]

The use of captured French vehicles extended beyond units involved in the invasion of Russia. To support Rommel's operations in North Africa, the German Army tried to purchase a large number of motor vehicles from the French. Owing to a variety of circumstances, however, the Germans only took delivery of about 1,500 trucks, of which some 400 were employed, mostly in North African ports because of a lack of spare parts.[82]

The panzer force ran into real problems, however, both before and during the invasion of the Soviet Union. First, the Germans realized that the majority of their tanks, mostly Pz Is and Pz IIs, were obsolete and had to be replaced by the more modern Pz III and Pz IV. The inability of German industry, however, to meet the unrealistic production quotas put forth by the responsible agencies and the expansion of the number of panzer and motorized infantry divisions meant that although the number of panzer divisions had doubled, Germany's total tank park remained static, as Figure 1.1 shows.[83]

Operation Barbarossa proved to be the beginning of the end for the German armor force. All the defects present in its equipment that proved to be minor problems in the 1939–1941 campaigns now became almost insurmountable obstacles. This started with the profusion of vehicle types and the use of captured material. The Wehrmacht entered the Soviet Union with over 2,000 different types of vehicles.[84] This even affected the organization of the German Army's cutting edge for the invasion, its four panzer groups. On 26 April 1941 Guderian sent a request to the Fourth Army asking that the 10th Panzer Division be allowed to remain with the Second Panzer Group, while the proposed transfer of the 8th Panzer Division to the Group be abandoned. One of the reasons Guderian cited was that the 8th was equipped with Czech material. Assigning the 8th Panzer division to his Panzer Group would violate the policy of equipping divisions within a group uniformly, thus creating supply and maintenance problems.[85] Guderian won his argument, as the 10th Panzer Division remained assigned to him, while the 8th Panzer Division went to the Fourth Panzer Group, part of Army Group North.[86] Likewise, most of the panzer and motorized infantry divisions equipped with French vehicles were assigned to General Hermann Hoth's Third Panzer Group, although Hoth later thought them poorly suited to operations in the east.[87]

Maintenance proved extremely difficult. Many of the French vehicles proved unsuitable to Russian conditions and large numbers quickly broke down. German wheeled vehicles also had tremendous difficulties, especially after the autumn rains turned roads into bottomless canals of mud. Captured Soviet trucks were too few and the Germans lacked both spare parts and repair facilities for them.[88] By the autumn, divisions such as the 11th Panzer were reporting serious shortages. By 16 October 1941, the 11th Panzer Division was short some 134 tanks and 427 other motor vehicles. The German Army had entered the Soviet Union on 22 June 1941 already short some 2,700 trucks.[89] Matters became worse as early as August when truck losses began to outrun production. The situation became catastrophic by late autumn. In November the Germans lost 5,996 trucks on the eastern front. This was double the production of 2,752 for the same month.[90]

The tank situation was equally bad. During 1941 tank production rose only marginally on a monthly basis, as Figure 1.2 shows. Once the campaign began in earnest, tank losses mounted and quickly began to outpace production, as Figures 1.3 and 1.4 demonstrate. Guderian noted the need for replacement engines by the mid summer of 1941. The best Hitler could do in the situation, however, was to promise 300 replacement engines for the entire eastern front in July.[91] Although tank strength fell during the battle of Kiev, the Panzer Groups were able to recover a fair degree of strength through strenuous maintenance efforts by the start of Operation Typhoon.[92]

The strains of the final lunge towards Moscow and the ensuing Soviet winter counteroffensive produced a severe crisis. By 10 December 1941, for example, divisions such as the 1st Panzer were reduced to just a handful of tanks. On 21 December 1941 the 10th Panzer Division's 7th Panzer Regiment had a total of 40 tanks, of which 25 were operational.[93] Transport was so short that divisions had to employ horse-drawn sleds and carts.[94] Equally worrisome was the nasty shock that was experienced by German tank crews when they met the Soviet T-34 medium and KV 1 heavy tanks. Although German intelligence may have been aware of the T-34 before the war, its existence was unknown to the troops in the field.[95] Although German tank crews had fought against technologically superior tanks in the 1940 French campaign, that quality never came into play, as the German Army was able to rapidly bring the campaign to a successful conclusion. The failure of Operation Barbarossa, however, presented the German Army with the prospect of fighting under conditions of both qualitative and quantitative inferiority for an extended period of time.

The passing of the winter crisis of 1941–1942 left the Germans with the problem of replacing losses. Halder realized as early as 10 December 1941 that it would not be possible to fully refit all of the panzer divisions.[96] This ultimately led to a reorganization of the panzer and motorized infantry divisions operating in Army Group South for the 1942 summer campaign. The Pz II was completely withdrawn from active service as obsolete, while Hitler agreed to the upgunning of both the Pz III and the Pz IV These changes, however necessary, did cause slowdowns in production, so that at a time when German tank production needed to increase dramatically, it did so only slightly, as Figure 1.2 shows.

The Germans also started the process for the production of two new tanks. The first was a design that had already been under consideration for some time. That was for a heavy tank that eventually became the Pz VI, or Tiger. The other was a medium tank designed to match the T-34. This eventually became the Pz V better known as the Panther. The history of these two vehicles is important because it illustrates the strengths and weaknesses of the panzer arm in its equipment and in terms of the German economy.

After seeing the competing designs for the Panther, Hitler decided on the model produced by the MAN company, which also produced railway equipment, and ordered production to begin in December 1942.[97] Two models of the Tiger were also produced in 1942. In this case, however, the two models were allowed to compete; one being built by the Henschel company, the other by one of Hitler's favorites, Professor Ferdinand Porsche.

The Panther went into production in January 1943, with the goal of producing 250 per month by May. This figure was slightly surpassed, but the entire first production series was insufficiently tested. Major defects were discovered at the front, especially in the steering mechanism. As a result, all 325 Panthers were withdrawn from service and sent to a specially constructed tank rebuilding plant outside Berlin.[98] In May they went out again and Army Group South employed some

200 Panthers at the battle of Kursk.[99] There they were a disappointment for a number of reasons. The Maybach HL 230 engine proved so unreliable that one battalion reported 25 engine failures in the space of only nine days. Problems with the engine persisted through the summer of 1943. Guderian formed a commission of inquiry to investigate, and the commission discovered a number of weaknesses in the engine that could not be corrected until January 1944 at the earliest.[100]

Even after the implementation of the commission's recommendations, the Panther remained mechanically unreliable. A report from the 1st SS Panzer Regiment dated 9 May 1944 indicated that almost as many Panthers were lost to breakdown as to enemy fire.[101] While the long 75mm gun proved devastatingly effective in combat, a poorly protected fuel injection system gave it a distressing tendency to burn when hit.[102] Interestingly, despite these problems, Guderian claimed to Hitler that the Panther, as well as the Tiger, were clearly superior to Russian and "Anglo-Saxon" tanks.[103]

Although the Panther went on to become one of, if not the best, medium tanks of the war, it was not really ready for combat service until late 1943 at the earliest. Even as favored a division as the 2nd SS Panzer Division (*Das Reich*), for example, did not employ Panthers in action until 1 September 1943.[104] The 1st Panzer Division did not get its Panthers until late October, while the 5th SS Panzer Division (*Wiking*) received its first Panthers at Kovel in April 1944.[105] Whatever qualitative advantage the Panther possessed was more than offset by much larger numbers of enemy tanks and by Germany's generally disastrous situation.

The Henschel Tiger first went into service in late 1942. It proved to be a superb machine, and proved effective until replaced by a slightly improved version popularly known as the Royal or King Tiger. The Tiger produced by Professor Porsche was another matter. A large investment in time, money and effort, it was officially adopted at Speer's speech of 22 November 1942.[106] The vehicle was employed at Kursk where it was a resounding failure. Although its gun was large enough to destroy any opposing armored vehicle, it had no secondary armament. Guderian, serving then as the Inspector General of Panzer Troops, noted its utter helplessness at Kursk when it had to go "quail shooting" with its gun against infantry.[107]

Even worse from the German standpoint was the production situation. German tank production for 1943 was based on the "Adolf Hitler Panzer Program," first presented by Speer at the aforementioned speech of 22 November 1942. Henschel Tiger production was set at 25 per month, rising to 50 by June 1943. Even these modest targets could not be met, and some disruptions were experienced due to the Allied strategic bombing offensive.[108] The problem faced by the economy and the air of unreality in which the German High Command lived is best illustrated by the following example. In early 1943, the Army General Staff recommended shutting down all tank production, and just building Panthers and Tigers exclusively. This would have included the upgunned version of the Panzer IV, which by that time had become the mainstay of the armor force. Guderian, then Inspector General of Panzer Troops, replied that if Panzer IV production was discontinued, Germany's entire tank production would consist of 25 Tigers a month, until Panther production could begin.[109] Even though he was well aware of these facts, Guderian was still proposing the creation of panzer divisions which would field 300–400 tanks each, a notion that can only be described as utterly ludicrous.[110]

Kursk is certainly regarded as the greatest tank battle in history, and often regarded as the swan song of the German armor force. Yet it is ironic to note that the German Army undertook its last great armored offensive in the east with an armor force that was largely obsolescent. Of the 2,700 tanks employed by the German Army in the attack, only a relatively small number were Panthers, and an even smaller proportion were Tigers. The majority consisted of versions of the Pz IV armed with the long 75mm gun. By the summer of 1943, however, the Pz IV had essentially reached the limit of its potential, and as such was barely a match for the T-34. There were also large numbers of Pz IIIs involved in the attack, including those armed with the short 50mm gun. The Pz III was by this time an obsolescent weapon, clearly inferior to the T-34 and the KV-1.[111] Thus, the German Army launched its last great attack in the east with a force that was qualitatively inferior.

By 1944 disruptions in production caused by the bombing, shortages of spare parts, and ever increasing combat losses all combined to vitiate the strength of the German panzer arm. On the eastern front, the shortage of spare parts came back to haunt the Germans. On 10 March 1944 units of Marshal Ivan S. Konev's 2nd Ukrainian Front captured the German supply depot of Uman, where they took some 300 immobilized German tanks. According to Army Group South, the tanks were damaged and could not be repaired because of a lack of spare parts. Evacuation of the tanks was impossible owing to the poor rail transport situation. Thus the tanks had to be left to the Soviets.[112]

Given the poor maintenance situation in the various theaters, especially on the eastern front, Hitler ordered in November 1943 that damaged tanks be sent back to Germany for repair. This way the tanks could be brought closer to the spare parts they needed. The effort, however, failed for several reasons. First, the maintenance performed in Germany proved no better than that performed at the front. Also, having the maintenance performed in Germany involved setting up a number of new organizations, thus consuming scarce men and resources. Finally, the delays involved in the process were monumental. Ordinarily, it would take about four weeks to get a damaged tank back to Germany. A further lengthy period would ensue before the repairs could be completed, followed by another four week journey back to the front. All of that could lead to a damaged tank being out of action for up to ten months! Guderian suggested that the best measure to solve this problem would be a steady supply of spare parts to the front.[113]

In the west, the crushing Allied air superiority made the movement of replacements to the front extremely difficult. Of all the panzer divisions in Normandy, by 8 July 1944 only the 21st Panzer Division, which had been in action since 6 June, had received any replacements for tanks and assault guns, and these amounted to only 17 Pz IVs.[114] Units such as SS General Josef "Sepp" Dietrich's I SS Panzer Corps, which had received no replacements at all as late as 18 July 1944, had to depend on the near heroic efforts of the corps tank repair and maintenance personnel on whom Dietrich showered praise and decorations.[115]

A problem of equal magnitude was the supply of spare parts. With German vehicles' carrying capacity being limited to begin with, and declining almost every day, spare parts had to take a back seat on the priority list compared to fuel and ammunition. This, however, created a shortage of spare parts. By 5 July 1944 the 2nd Panzer Division, which had been in action since 9 June 1944, regarded the supply of spare parts as critical to the division's ability to undertake combat operations in the near future.[116]

The vehicle situation was equally poor. Panzer divisions on all fronts were reporting a variety of problems with vehicles. Some divisions had to make do with aged vehicles. The 8th Panzer Division, for example, had not had a refit since 1941. This put the division in a situation where only part of the division's infantry could be motorized. The 23rd Panzer Division, created in 1942, reported in August 1944 that all of its vehicles had been driven over 12,000 miles.[117] Likewise, the lst Panzer Division, after a month of hard combat in southern Poland with the III Panzer Corps, reported that by the end of July 1944, only 29% of its truck carrying capacity was ready for action.[118] In the west, before the Normandy invasion, OKW decided that its reserve of 3,000 trucks would be assigned to refitting panzer divisions to restore their mobility, in addition, such dispersion removed the vehicles from a relatively confined area where they were vulnerable to air attack.[119]

The cause of many of the vehicle problems facing the divisions related to tires. Rubber was always in short supply in Germany, and the war only worsened the situation. Attempts were made to expand the production of synthetic rubber, Buna, and recycling drives were undertaken. In their efforts the Germans were aided by the Japanese, who sent some small amounts of raw rubber by submarine. This made the production of Buna possible, as it required a small amount of raw rubber as a base.[120]

The Germans made attempts to stretch, so to speak, their stock of tires by repairing them with rubber cement and rubber stain.[121] All these efforts, however, proved of no avail. The *Panzer Lehr* Division, for example, reported that before the invasion of Normandy most accidents involving wheeled vehicles were caused by worn or defective tires.[122] Matters were made worse by the fact that supplies often had to be driven to the units over long distances, thus increasing the wear and tear on the already worn out tires.[123]

The situation on the eastern front was just as bad. The 12th Panzer Division, part of Army Group North, reported in August that its reconnaissance vehicles lacked tires.[124] In fact by August 1944 panzer divisions all over the eastern front were reporting serious shortages of tires.[125]

The invasion of Normandy combined with defeats in Italy and the eastern front to drive losses up to catastrophic levels. During the first twenty-four days of the Normandy invasion, the Germans lost some 2,400 vehicles, including 1,866 trucks.[126] In the aftermath of the breakout from St. Lo and the Falaise disaster, vehicle losses swelled to about 20,000.[127] Ghastly losses were suffered at the same time on the eastern front, where Army Group Center was obliterated by the Soviet summer offensive. In fact, German truck losses from January to August 1944 were over 109,000, the equivalent of the entire 1943 production.[128] The 1944 production could not nearly keep up with this. Under the impact of heavy losses some divisions, such as the 20th Panzer and the 13th Panzer, resorted to the common expedient of using horses for transport.[129]

Germany's oil situation deteriorated steadily during the war. Already dependent on Romania for oil before the war, the outbreak of hostilities only increased it. The victorious campaigns of 1939 and 1940 did nothing to relieve Germany's oil problem. On 28 November 1940 the Army High Command (OKH) reported to the Armed Forces High Command (OKW) that the newly established monthly allocations of gasoline and diesel fuel were wholly inadequate to meet the needs of even relatively minor operations such as the projected invasion of Greece.[130]

Germany increased its oil imports from Romania to 2,114,000 tons by 1941. This proved totally inadequate to meet the requirements for the 1941 campaign against the Soviet Union, forcing the Germans to conduct Operation Barbarossa on what amounted to a logistical shoestring.[131] To make up for shortfalls in oil production the civilian populations, especially in the occupied countries, would have to made sacrifices. On 23 July 1942, for example, Göring wrote to Hans Frank, the Governor-General of Poland, demanding that the Polish civil population drastically cut its oil consumption so more oil could be diverted to the German military.[132] Indeed, it was the demand for oil that led Hitler to undertake the ill-fated Stalingrad campaign.

By 1944 Germany's oil situation was desperate. The oil campaign carried out by the Allied air forces in mid 1944 greatly affected Germany's synthetic oil production.[133] Allied bombing attacks also seriously damaged the Romanian oil industry. Romanian oil production fell from 5,665,357 tons in 1942 to 5,273,432 tons in 1943.[134] German and Romanian officials did plan to expand drilling in the Romanian oil fields in 1944. In addition, there were plans to modernize Romanian facilities and improve the transportation situation to make the oil more accessible.[135]

All these plans, however, came to naught. During the first five months of 1944, Romanian oil targets remained a very high priority for the Allied air forces, especially the American Fifteenth Air Force in Italy. By the middle of May 1944 Romania's crude oil output had been reduced by 44%, with an even greater reduction in the output of refined oil. During the first ten days in May alone, damage to refineries, rail sidings and pipelines resulted in the loss of 53,000 tons of oil. The refineries at Ploesti and Campina, as well as the rail lines at Bucharest and Ploesti, had been seriously damaged. Likewise, storage tanks and pipelines had sustained considerable damage. The German commander at Ploesti, Luftwaffe Lieutenant General Alfred Gerstenberg, energetically undertook a number of measures to improve the situation. These ranged from strengthening the anti-aircraft and fighter defenses to bomb proofing storage facilities, as well as repairing rail lines. It was felt that these measure could restore the situation, but only if there were no further air attacks and nothing was done that would threaten the supply lines of Army Group South Ukraine.[136] Neither the American Fifteenth Air Force nor the Soviets would prove so obliging. A great deal of oil traffic from Romania to Germany traveled via the Danube River. The Royal Air Force Bomber Command was able to disrupt this traffic by heavily mining the river.[137] The Germans ultimately lost their most important source of oil when Romania changed sides on 23 August 1944.

Efforts were made to compensate for the lack of oil. The Army, for example, tried to adapt vehicles to run on wood alcohol, an effort that ultimately proved unsuccessful. On 29 May 1944 the quartermaster of Army Group B noted that of the 14,578 trucks in the Seventh and Fifteenth Armies, only 3,552 had been converted to run on wood alcohol.[138]

The Economics Ministry also undertook to keep the Wehrmacht supplied with oil. The RWM developed a plan in the summer of 1944 to disperse oil producing and refining facilities, while increasing gasoline production to 124,000 tons per month and diesel fuel to 80,000 tons per month.[139] The RWM also tried to develop some alternative sources of oil, the most notable of which was Austria. In January 1945, Austria provided some 286,962 liters of gasoline to Germany. The effort to develop Austria as a source of oil, however, ultimately proved a failure owing to shortages of coal, cement and motor oil. There were also problems in moving oil from the drilling sites to the refining facilities.[140] Even before interest in Austria arose, the RWM also explored the possibility of developing Serbia and Croatia as oil sources. Both did produce oil, but in amounts too small to be of any significance.[141] Likewise efforts were made to expand oil production in Hungary, which after Romania was Germany's main source of oil. Hungarian oil production, however, was generally only about 20% of Romania's production.[142] Even if these efforts had been successful, it would still have been too little, too late.

The increasing shortage of oil had two major effects on the Army in general and the panzer arm in particular. Owing to fuel shortages, many units had little tactical mobility. The panzer and panzer grenadier units of the Second Army, for example, part of Army Group Center, could only move short distances because of a lack of fuel. This left it poorly prepared to fend off the impending Soviet 1944 summer offensive that would ultimately annihilate Army Group Center.[143] For units that were not in action, such as the 11th Panzer Division, awaiting the invasion of southern France in July 1944, the lack of fuel also has an impact. The division could not conduct unit training or additional training for tank commanders because of fuel shortages.[144]

The failure of the German economy to keep the panzer arm adequately supplied with equipment forced important changes in the organization of both panzer and panzer grenadier divisions. The most important of these was the mere existence of such divisions. Since the vast majority of the German Army's tractive power was based on horses, tanks and vehicles had to be concentrated into a few special divisions, which in turn were concentrated into corps. To have done anything else under the circumstances would have been foolish in the extreme.

Another manifestation of German economic inadequacy, as well as the impact of rising losses, was the inability to adequately equip new armored formations, as well as the reduction of authorized tank strength in divisions during the war. An OKH Organization Section study on armaments for 1944 made it quite clear that by the end of 1944, the Army hoped to have available 32 panzer divisions, each with 130 tanks, based on a combination of Pz IVs and Panthers, plus 12 to 14 Tiger battalions. To achieve this, German industry would have to produce 400 Pz IVs, 400 Panthers and 130 Tigers per month.[145] These figures were never met, and the number of real panzer divisions never exceeded 30.[146]

Authorized tank strength in divisions declined as the war went on. In 1939, German tank companies had an authorized tank strength of 22, but by 1943 this was reduced to 17. In the case of panzer grenadier divisions, tank companies were authorized 14 tanks. Very often assault guns were used in lieu of tanks.[147] This was essentially a tank gun mounted in a turretless hull on a tank chassis. They were originally designed by Erich von Manstein to provide armored support to infantry divisions.[148]

The increasing reliance on assault guns as an economically feasible substitute for tanks was bitterly opposed by Guderian in his capacity as Inspector General of Panzer Troops.[149] To be sure, there was a bureaucratic aspect to this. From their inception, assault guns came under the purview of the artillery branch, not the armor branch. Guderian, who was every bit as much a bureaucratic infighter and empire builder as any other major figure in the Third Reich, eventually did succeed in late 1943 in gaining control over these vehicles.[150] There was also a doctrinal aspect to the panzer leader's position, which will be discussed in another chapter.

Despite Guderian's criticism, assault guns had a great many things in their favor. First, they were cheaper to build. Also, the lack of a turret proved an advantage in installing a heavier gun without adding a prohibitive amount of weight to the vehicle. Being essentially much simpler vehicles, assault guns had higher readiness rates than tanks, even when the total tank and assault gun parks reached comparable size late in the war, as a comparison of Figures 1.10 and 1.11 clearly demonstrates. The lack of a turret was a tactical drawback as it gave the gun only a very limited traverse of 24 degrees as opposed to a tank's 360 degree traverse, a fact that was already noted by both proponents and opponents of them.[151]

Despite Guderian's worries, assault guns never threatened the primacy of the tank as the panzer arm's premier weapon. Germany's assault gun production and park only approached equality with that of the tank in the fall of 1944 and very early 1945, as a comparison of Figures 1.1, 1.2, 1.5 and 1.6 clearly indicates. In addition, the vast majority of assault guns were sent to the infantry divisions, as was the original intent behind them.[152]

Tiger tanks were relatively rare, and they were used mainly as corps or army assets, although the Army's elite *Gross Deutschland* Division did have an organic battalion of Tigers.[153] A Tiger company was normally authorized only 10 tanks, but this became true of all tank companies in 1945.

Captured equipment was still used, and captured factories were employed to fill the needs of divisions in local areas. In Italy, for example, the Germans used the Ansaldo-Fiat works to produce several types of assault guns, reconnaissance cars and other vehicles. They were sent to units in either Italy or the Balkans.[154] In the west, the 21st Panzer Division, although equipped with Pz IVs and assault guns, had to use a large quantity of French equipment.[155]

The SS formations, being somewhat more favored in terms of equipment, had both infantry regiments of most of their panzer divisions equipped with half-tracks, while the rest used wheeled transport.[156] This practice was also abandoned by late 1944 because of equipment shortfalls. The 1st SS Panzer Division (*Adolf Hitler*) had to employ a "mixed" tank battalion, consisting half of tanks and half of infantry mounted in half-tracks.[157] The Inspector General of Panzer Troops eventually advocated panzer divisions using this kind of organization in the panzer regiment.[158] The lack of vehicles generally mandated the use of horses for transport for Army panzer divisions, and they were probably used by the SS as well.[159]

The constant cuts in vehicle strength clearly impaired the fighting efficiency of the panzer force. By 1943 divisions rarely came up to strength, especially in transport. This could severely impact the supporting arms in divisions. The 1st Panzer Division, for example, even with a slightly improved vehicle situation in July 1944, lacked the transport capability to tow the 88 mm guns of the 299th Army Flak Battalion, which had recently been assigned to the division.[160] Matters were made worse by the loss rate suffered as a result of the increasing tempo of combat operations as the war went on.

Services often measure success or failure by the rate of loss suffered by the units involved. Air forces, for example, during World War II considered a loss rate of 5% on a mission basis to be prohibitive over the long run.[161] Although no rate of loss on a monthly basis was apparently ever established by any army, it might be possible to arrive at a figure by the following procedure. That would be to look at the monthly tank and assault gun losses as a percentage of the total tank and assault gun parks, and then compare that rate to the corresponding success or failure encountered by the army in its campaigns. The figure would tend to indicate that in periods of crisis or defeat, losses ran at a monthly rate of about 10% or more of the total park, as indicated in Figures 1.8 and 1.9.

This rate would be affected by several things. First, it must be realized that one of the most important things in making losses good is the ability to move replacements to the front. The Germans were hindered in this on both eastern and western fronts. On the eastern front, they could never solve the logistical problems created by the paucity of rail lines and the problem of converting the Russian rail lines to the standard European gauge. On the western front, the ability to move replacements to the front was rendered almost impossible by Allied air interdiction. Matters were made worse, from the German standpoint, by the defensive nature of the war in its later stages. From 1943 on the Germans fought in battles that often resulted in retreats. This deprived them of the primary prerequisites for efficient field maintenance, control of the battlefield. German field maintenance units themselves were also badly mauled in these circumstances. In Normandy, for example, by 14 June 1944 the 21st Panzer Division had only two 18 ton prime movers available for salvage operations. The *Panzer Lehr* Division's salvage platoon was operating at only 40% effectiveness due to losses.[162] The lack of vehicles in general made the German armies more vulnerable to the better equipped Allied and Soviet armies. This was certainly the case on both the western front in France and on the eastern front during the destruction of Army Group Center.

In conclusion, it is obvious that Germany did not possess the type of economy necessary to the creation and maintenance of a large armored force. The German steel and oil industries were clearly incapable of providing for the needs of three services.[163] In this context Hitler's decision to proceed with the construction of large capital ships must be viewed as a serious error. While it was understandable in the sense of Hitler's desires in regard to Britain and eventually the United States, it displayed a complete lack of understanding of the relationship between ends and means in regards to Germany's continental opponents. Even if the requisite number of tanks and vehicles could have been produced, Germany's synthetic oil production and the importation of Romanian oil was insufficient to support Germany's armored force. The inability of the German economy to keep the Army as a whole modernly equipped forced the Army into the unsatisfactory expedient of using foreign equipment as well as a heavy reliance on horses for transport. This dependence increased as battlefield reverses created shortages of both vehicles and gasoline. Ultimately, the best way to describe the panzer arm in the context of the German Army as a whole is that in a technological sense, it was the only part of the Army that was more clearly related to the twentieth century than the nineteenth.

Figure 1.1
Tank Park, 1941–1945

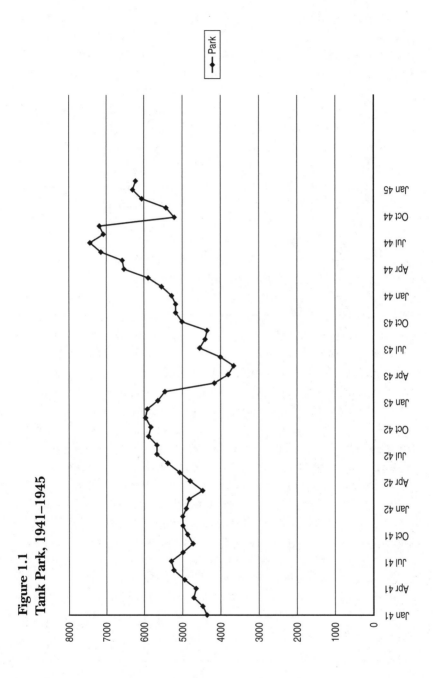

Figure 1.2
Tank Production, 1941–1945

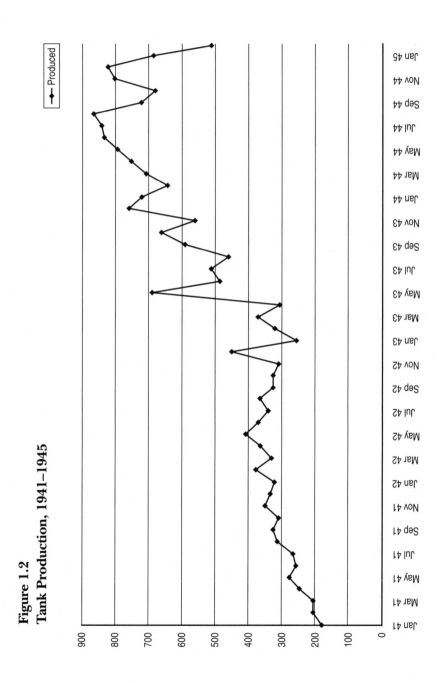

Figure 1.3
Tank Losses, 1941–1945

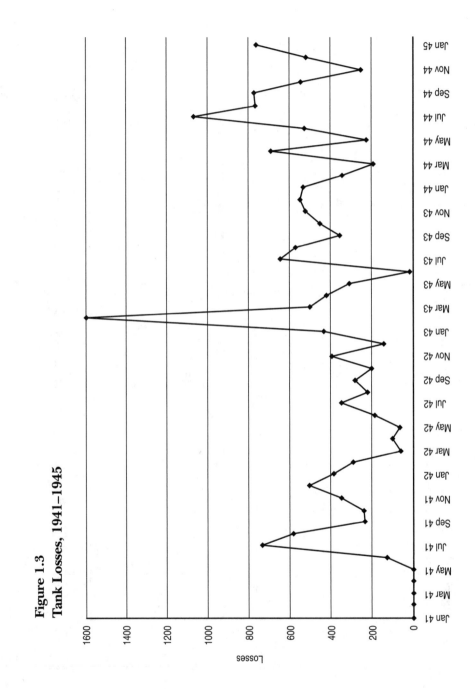

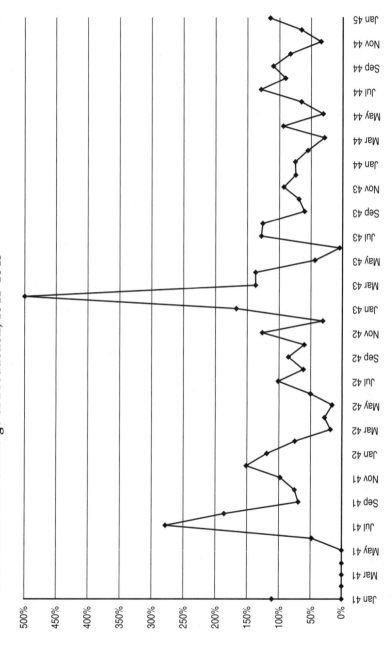

Figure 1.4
Tank Losses as a Percentage of Production, 1941–1945

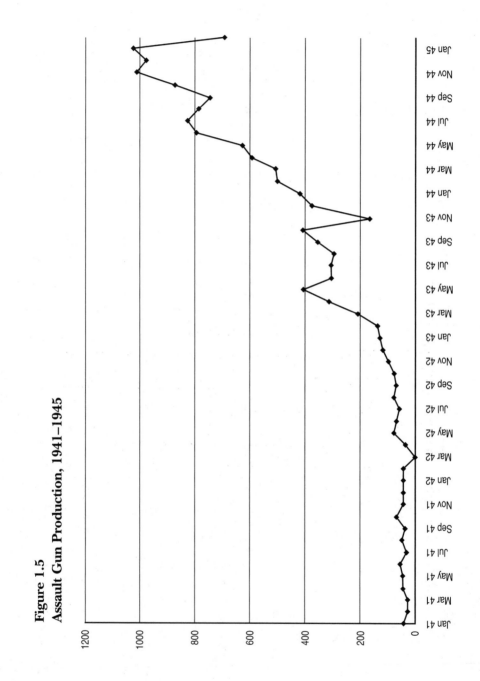

Figure 1.5
Assault Gun Production, 1941–1945

Figure 1.6
Assault Gun Park, 1941–1945

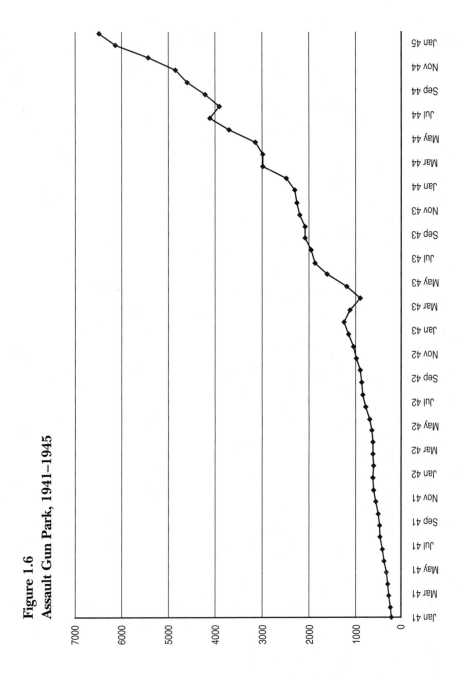

Figure 1.7
Assault Gun Losses, 1941–1945

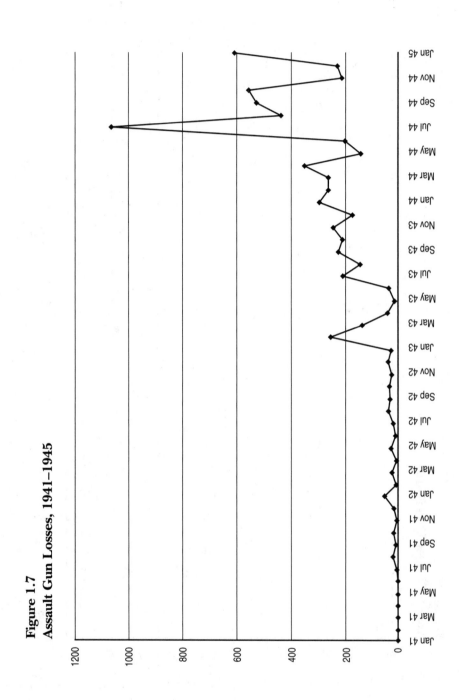

Figure 1.8
Tank Losses as a Percentage of Park, 1941–1945

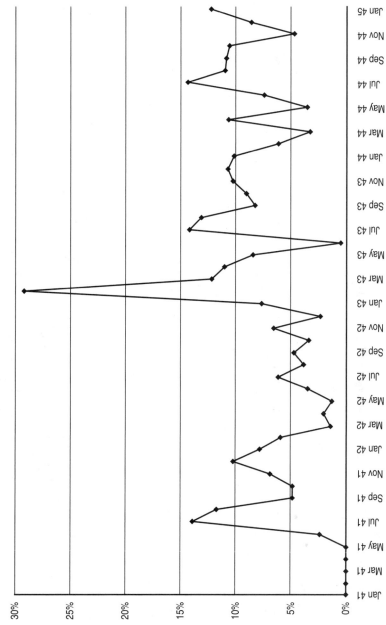

Figure 1.9
Assault Gun Losses as a Percentage of Park, 1941–1945

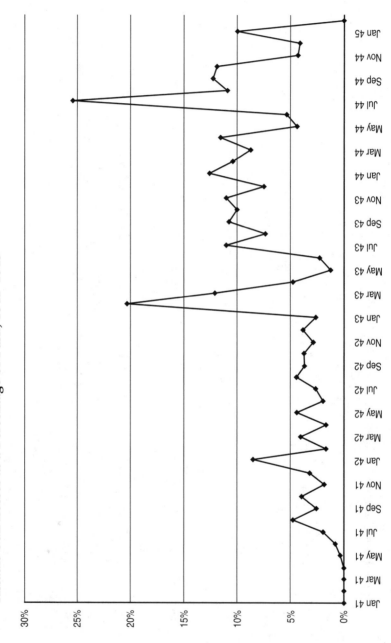

Figure 1.10
Tank Readiness Rates, 1941–1945

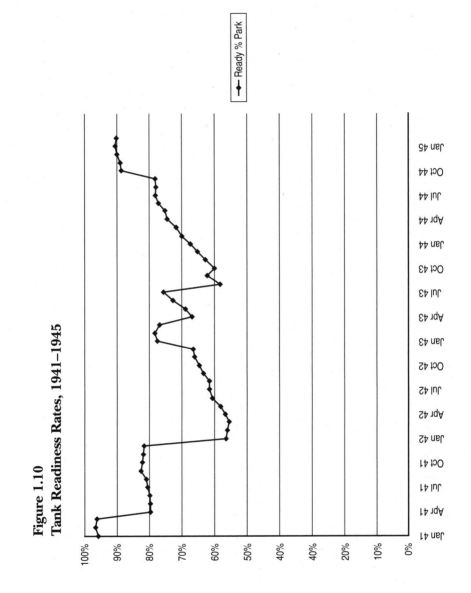

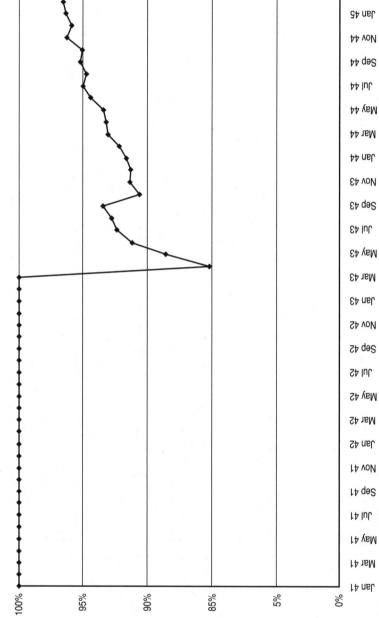

Figure 1.11
Assault Gun Readiness Rates, 1941–1945

CHAPTER TWO

Personnel Policies and the Panzer Arm

"What is there to say? Can anyone understand, can anyone imagine what Germany's finest men have done in this war."

—WILHELM PRÜLLER[1]

"Only the old soldiers, who experienced the victorious battles of earlier years, who on the basis of their experience have more understanding of the 'situation,' feel superior to the Russians. They are those who keenly help the Lieutenants or NCOs in the attack, and who give support in the defense."

—20TH PANZER DIVISION, 1944[2]

In spite of all the technological improvements in weaponry, equipment and communications, war is still a human activity. People are generally a country's most important resource, and how this resource is used will affect a country's performance in war, and Germany was no exception to this rule. In examining Germany's use of manpower, one should answer the following questions. What kind of population did Germany have? What were the conscription policies of Hitler's regime? What were the procedures for processing wounded men and incorporating replacements into units? How did these things influence the panzer arm's performance? Some of these matters have been covered to some degree in Martin van Creveld's work *Fighting Power*, and this chapter will rely to some degree on that work in some areas, while other areas will be explored in greater depth here.

An armored force is based heavily on machines, but machines are both operated and repaired by people. Thus one of the most important prerequisites for the creation of a large armored force is an automotively inclined population; that is, a population that has extensive contact with automobiles, trucks, or any other automotive devices. Perhaps the best way to examine such an inclination in a country's population is to look at the number of people per vehicle in a country. A low number would indicate a population that is well-acquainted with motor vehicles, while a high number would indicate just the opposite. By this standard, Germany was in a very backward state. In a 1935 article, Guderian stated that in 1933 there was one commercially or privately owned vehicle for every five people in the United States, while there was one vehicle for every seventy-five people in Germany.[3] In fact, the true state of affairs was much worse than Guderian believed. In 1933 the ratio was actually one vehicle for every eighty-nine people. Although strenuous efforts reduced this ratio by 1937 to one vehicle for every forty-seven people, it was still the poorest ratio in western Europe, with the exception of Italy.[4] Thus Germany did not have the type of population conducive to the creation of a large armored or motorized force. This, along with several other factors to be discussed later, caused shortages of drivers and personnel for salvage and maintenance operations.

Perhaps the most important phase in a soldier's training is his initial conscription and classification, for it is at this point that an army can exert an important influence on his subsequent career. In Germany, this even involved the service a male of military age went into, because in Germany there were no all-volunteer services. In Germany the three services got a pre-determined share of the manpower available for that year. When the class of 1920, for example, was drafted in 1940 the total number of men available for military service was 520,739. Of these, some 377,536, or 72.5%, went into the Army. The Luftwaffe got the next highest share, 114,562 men, or 21.9% of the total. The Navy took only 22,913 men, a mere 4.4%. The SS was low on the totem pole, getting 5,728 men, or 1.2%. The SS also received further compensation from the other three services. The Army had to give up 7,322 men, or 1.9% of its share. The Luftwaffe also gave up 1.9% of its share, some 2,223 men. Even the Navy had to give up 445 men to the SS. All of the services also recruited volunteers.[5]

Induction into one of the armed services often depended on the organization one belonged to as a child or as an adolescent. From early on there was cooperation between the Hitler Youth and the commanders of the Army Military Districts (*Wehrkreise*).[6] In fact a comparison of the maps showing the boundaries of the various Wehrkreise and the "Hitler Youth Regions" (*Hitler Jugendgebieten*) reveals an almost exact correspondence. The only exceptions were the larger *Wehrkreise*, which incorporated two *Hitler Jugendgebieten*. The Hitler Youth itself was not a homogeneous organization, but was divided into flying units, naval units, and so on.[7] A youth from one of these organizations was likely to wind up in either the Luftwaffe or the Navy.

For the panzer arm, the two most important organizations were the motorized units of the Hitler Youth and the National Socialist Motor Corps (*Nationalsozialistisches Kraftkorps*, or NSKK). The motorized Hitler Youth expanded from 3,000 members in 1933 to 102,000 in 1938. Training in this organization included both driving and mechanics. A member was generally given eighty hours of driving time and 105 hours of training as a mechanic. The motorized Hitler Youth was initially only supposed to supply personnel to other Nazi Party organizations, especially the NSKK. Only later were members of the motorized Hitler Youth sent directly to the Army or the SS.[8]

The NSKK took over the training of members of the motorized Hitler Youth after they had passed out of the Hitler Youth. Between 1933 and 1939 the NSKK trained 187,000 drivers for the Army.[9] The NSKK also trained personnel for maintenance shops and repair units.

A person's civilian occupation also tended to determine one's branch of service. The Luftwaffe, for example, in its formative stages drew personnel from Germany's national air-line, Lufthansa, although civilian flying experience did not automatically qualify a person to fly a military aircraft.[10] The Army made a similar error in drafting auto mechanics directly into tank maintenance units, where they proved a liability in combat situations because they lacked military training.[11]

Once drafted into the service, a soldier would then be carefully examined by a physician and his prospective regimental commander. The outcome of these interviews would ultimately determine the soldier's branch of service. On the basis of these interviews, for example, Karl Fuchs, a young Franconian draftee, was selected to be a tank gunner.[12] The soldier would then be sent to the replacement battalion of his division that was part of the Replacement Army. He would then undergo training at the necessary schools required for his position, and then eventually be posted to a "march battalion," which would take the replacements *en masse* to the parent unit. There the battalion would be broken up and the men assigned to their proper units by the regimental or battalion commanders.

Like its imperial predecessor, the German Army's divisions were organized on a territorial basis. The personnel came from the same territorial area, or even a large city such as Vienna or Berlin. The 1st Panzer Division, for example, was based in Thuringia, with most of its units being divided between Erfurt and Weimar.[13] As the total number of Wehrkreise increased with Germany's territorial acquisitions during the 1930s, the Army would often post divisions to a new *Wehrkreis* to tap into newly available sources of manpower. The 2nd Panzer Division, for example, was originally German. After the *Anschluss*, however, the division was posted to Austria, so that by 1944 its personnel consisted almost entirely of Austrians.[14] This, incidentally, caused the Americans, mistakenly as it turned out, to rate the division as being of poor quality.

The territorial system provided the Germans with several advantages. First, the system was very cognizant of the psychological needs of the fighting soldier. This contributed to the cohesion of German units in combat.[15] Strenuous efforts were made to maintain the integrity of the units. This even involved pulling whole divisions out of the front line for rehabilitation, the careful treatment of replacements and the wounded, as well as the granting of leave. The authority for the conduct of these policies was generally left in the hands of the officers of the units concerned.[16]

The treatment of the wounded was very important. The basic German policy was to return wounded men to their old units. For this purpose, divisions often established their own convalescent homes. Here, usually under the supervision of non-commissioned officers (NCOs), men would engage in a variety of activities, including sports, to begin the process of getting the men back into suitable physical condition.[17]

The German policy of returning wounded soldiers to their old units was important in two respects. First, from the point of view of the individual soldier, it was important that he return to the familiar surroundings and comradeship afforded by his old unit. This helped lessen the strain that the soldier would have to face upon his reentry into combat.[18] In a larger sense, returning wounded represented to their old unit a badly needed reservoir of experience which could be used to leaven the rest of the division's manpower. This was especially true for units that were rebuilding or refitting. In the spring of 1944, for example, the 2nd Panzer Division was refitting in France. While the division had its full complement of authorized enlisted men, it was short some 54 officers and 800 NCOs. The Army Personnel Office would handle the matter of assigning officers, while the deficit in NCOs would be closed by the incorporation of NCOs returning from convalescence.[19] The combat experience these NCOs brought with them was vital in enabling the young, inexperienced replacements to withstand the shock of the introduction to combat.[20]

The granting of leave was also given high priority. Fighting units regularly granted leave to soldiers as a matter of policy. A good example of this come from the diary of Wilhelm Prüller, a sergeant in the 9th Panzer Division. During the winter crisis after the failure of Operation Typhoon in December 1941, Prüller was denied leave at Christmas by his company commander, Lieutenant Hans Eichert. When the crisis passed, however, Eichert made sure that Prüller got three weeks leave in March 1942.[21] This policy was maintained by the Sixth Army, even while it was under the strain of the Stalingrad campaign.[22] Policies such as these were instrumental in building and maintaining a division's *Kampfkraft*, or fighting power, and in keeping the number of psychological casualties to a minimum.

The Germans went to such pains in their personnel policies because the German Army believed in the idea of quality over quantity. The experience of both World War I and World War II as it progressed indicated that the outcome of a battle could be determined by the actions of small units with a few well-trained and experienced soldiers, NCOs and officers.[23] Given the fact that, especially in the later stages of the war, the German Amy was fighting under conditions of numerical inferiority, it was considered vital to have some "old hands" around. Men who were veterans of the victorious campaigns of the 1939–1942 period were considered especially valuable. They could set the example for the younger soldiers, who might be intimidated by the numerical superiority of the Russians.[24]

On the western front, the commander of the *Panzer Lehr* Division, Fritz Bayerlein, urged the relief of his division in August 1944 after some sixty days of combat. One of the factors Bayerlein cited was that if the division was pulled out of the line now, the remaining panzer grenadiers could be saved. These men had accumulated a wealth of combat experience which would be vital in allowing the division to regain its old combat value.[25]

The Germans also determined on the basis of personnel whether or not to rebuild a destroyed division. A comparison of the fate of the panzer divisions lost at Stalingrad and the 10th Panzer Division provides an excellent example of this.

The German Sixth Army contained three panzer divisions, the 14th, 16th and 24th. All of them were rebuilt after their destruction at Stalingrad. The 14th, for example, was able to draw on personnel from several sources. First, not all of the division was in Stalingrad when the Sixth Army was surrounded. Elements of it were attached to Lieutenant General Ferdinand Heim's XLVIII Panzer Corps, which was the mobile reserve behind the Romanian Third Army on the Don, and so escaped encirclement.[26] The division's replacement battalion was still functioning in Germany and could provide men. The division had been in combat for an extended period of time and had accumulated a large number of wounded who were at rear area hospitals. These men would be sent to the replacement battalion in Germany and then on to the division itself after their recovery. Some men would also have been obtained from those flown out of Stalingrad. During the Luftwaffe's effort to supply the surrounded Sixth Army, about 32,000 men were flown out of the city; almost 25,000 wounded and about 7,000 "specialists." The latter included people ranging from general officers to drivers and maintenance personnel from panzer units.[27] Also, since German divisions granted leave even in the most trying circumstances, there would have been a number of men on leave when the division was encircled in November 1942. Thus, there were enough men around to reconstitute the division.

The 10th Panzer Division had been severely battered in the 1941 Russian campaign. It spent 1942 rebuilding in France and participated in the occupation of Vichy France. In December of 1942 it was deployed to Tunisia, and fought there until the surrender on 13 May 1943. The 19th Panzer Division was not rebuilt because the manpower sources available to the 14th Panzer Division were not available to the 10th. Since the Axis supply line to North Africa became extremely tenuous, it was impossible to evacuate the wounded or send soldiers out on leave. Thus there were not enough cadre personnel to rebuild the division after it had been destroyed. Indeed, it is interesting to note that while the 10th Panzer Division was not rebuilt, the other two panzer divisions with long service in North Africa, the 15th and 21st, were rebuilt. Both of these divisions had been in North Africa for two years and had been receiving replacements by airlift.[28] Having been there for an extended period of time, they were thus able to develop the same sources of manpower available to divisions such as the 14th Panzer. Additionally, the German forces in North Africa had to send some 17,000 men back to Germany in August of 1942. These were men who, while fit for duty in Europe, were no longer able to withstand the rigors of tropical service.[29] At least some of these men would have been available to these units when they were later rebuilt. The 21st also received men in its reconstitution who had seen combat service in the Soviet Union, and in an organizational sense, was something of a hybrid.[30] The 21st Panzer Division was reformed in the summer of 1943, while the 15th Panzer Division was reformed as the 15th Panzer Grenadier Division due to equipment shortages.[31]

When the Germans did reconstitute a division from scratch, it generally took about three months to assemble the requirement personnel. On 23 March 1943, the 14th Panzer Division reported its strength as 78 officers, 1,054 NCOs, and 4,271 men.[32] By 20 June 1943 the division had 282 officers, 2,181 NCOs, and 9,450 men, close to deployable strength.[33] The war diary of the 24th Panzer Division gives an almost identical story.[34]

All this, however, is not to say that the Germans always used their manpower wisely. When the Army expanded during the 1930s, it had to rely on the classes of 1914–1917, which were relatively small owing to the depressed birthrate encountered during World War I. The number of men available in these classes was made smaller still by the fact that a substantial number of them had been trained as skilled workers in armaments industries and therefore could not be drafted.[35] In addition to this, although more use of women in the work force was made than was previously thought, a large number of men were also kept on in nonessential factories, a fact which Halder found extremely irritating.[36]

Another potentially large source of manpower was wasted in the creation of the Luftwaffe Field Divisions. By 1942 mounting aircraft losses had created a large surplus of ground personnel for the Luftwaffe, a potentially important source of replacements for the Army. They would have been particularly important for the panzer arm, as the Luftwaffe's ground elements were fully motorized. Thus these men represented a potential source of drivers, mechanics and maintenance personnel. "Der Dicke," however, was in no mind to let his dedicated National Socialists fall into the corrupting clutches of the decadent Army.[37] The Luftwaffe began deploying Luftwaffe Field Divisions in late 1942, rising to twenty-one divisions by 1 July 1943.[38] In combat, these divisions proved a complete waste, often shattering almost immediately after entering combat. As a result, many highly skilled men who could have been of great value to both the Army and the Luftwaffe were lost.[39] They became an additional drain on the Army when the Army had to provide officers and NCOs to these useless formations. Eventually, most of them were disbanded, although there were still eleven Luftwaffe Field Divisions in the German order of battle by 31 July 1944.[40] Wasteful policies such as these combined with steady combat losses to place a serious drain on the Army's available manpower.

The recruitment of personnel for the SS divisions was quite different from that of the Army. The SS was a volunteer organization, although it did have access to about 1% of the Army's annual draft.[41] The SS generally obtained its members from other Nazi Party organizations. An agreement between Reichsführer SS Heinrich Himmler and Hitler Youth Leader Baldur von Schirach, dated 17 December 1938, essentially made the Hitler Youth Land Service a replacement organization for the SS.[42] Members of the General SS were also liable to service in SS combat formations. Some divisions even had special sources of men. The *Totenkopf* Division, for example, was staffed by personnel drawn from the guard detachments of concentration camps.[43] This, plus the activities of Himmler's chief recruiter Gottlob Berger, actually gave the *Totenkopf* a considerable surplus of men over its authorized strength.[44]

The relatively meager supply of indigenous manpower available to the SS was sufficient, however, for their units only up through the end of the French campaign. The expansion of the SS from two to five divisions, directed by Hitler on 21 February 1941, called for a much larger supply of men.[45] The SS was able to accomplish this without the use of foreign manpower, as SS training schools had been able to produce a surplus of soldiers, especially officers.[46] This was vital to the success of the expansion of the SS. Unlike their Army counterparts, SS divisions had no territorial affiliation. Rather, their *esprit de corps* was based on a combination of ideological training and a firm belief that they were the elite of the Nazi movement.

The SS faced a serious manpower shortage, however, due to high combat losses. Between 1 September 1939 and 1 March 1942, the SS lost 14,213 men killed or missing and 35,576 men wounded.[47] To offset these losses, the SS staged a massive recruiting drive in Germany to lure draft age men from the Army into the SS. Another source of recruits was foreign manpower.

After the start of Operation Barbarossa, a substantial recruiting campaign was initiated in foreign countries, the theme being that Europeans should participate in a "crusade against Bolshevism."[48] For purposes of allocation, foreign volunteers were classified into two broad categories. Germanic volunteers consisted of Danes, Finns, Flems, Dutch, Swedes and Norwegians, who were allocated to the SS. Non-Germanic volunteers, including French, Coats, Spaniards and Walloons, were normally assigned to the Army.[49] These volunteers were quickly accepted. Between 22 June and 19 September 1941, the 5th SS Division (*Wiking*) incorporated 2,559 Germanic volunteers into its units. These included 1,452 Dutch, 585 Norwegians, 467 Danes, 45 Flems, 9 Swedes and a single Swiss volunteer. Given this mix of nationalities, it was not surprising that some units experienced communication problems.[50] By the time the *Wiking* Division was upgraded to a full panzer division in 1943, its personnel were almost entirely foreign.

As combat losses mounted, greater and greater use was made of non-German manpower by both services. The SS continued to make use of "Germanic" volunteers, going so far as to recruit former Danish soldiers who had been demobilized after the occupation of Denmark in 1940, and creating a separate Norwegian unit.[51] By 1943 the SS began to raise formations composed of ethnic groups hitherto excluded, such as the French and Croats. A French SS infantry division, the 33rd SS Division (*Charlemagne*), even participated in the defense of Berlin.[52]

The best of the SS panzer divisions, the 1st, 2nd, 3rd, 9th, 10th and 12th, were kept as German as possible. The SS also tried to increase its quota of German manpower and did so, but not without strenuous objections from the Army. In 1943, for example, the SS wanted to draft a minimum of 60,000 men from the class of 1925, while the Army declared this to be the absolute maximum the SS could take. In this case, the question was resolved in the Army's favor, as it was decided that giving the SS that many recruits from the Army would deprive the Army of too many potential NCOs and junior officers.[53]

In view of the restrictions on SS recruiting in Germany, the SS relied heavily on the *Volksdeutsche*, ethnic Germans who lived outside of Germany. Himmler found very good hunting in this respect in the *Volksdeutsche* communities of Czechoslovakia, Hungary and Romania.[54] Their use even extended to the most Germanic of the SS panzer divisions. While reforming in early 1944, the 2nd SS Panzer Division (*Das Reich*) received some 9,000 replacements, many of whom were Alsatians and *Volksdeutsche*.[55] This applied to other SS panzer divisions as well. The 3rd Division (*Totenkopf*), while still a motorized infantry division, had to use *Volksdeutsche* recruits as replacements as early as 1941, as a result of the high losses suffered in combat in the Barbarossa campaign. The division commander, the notorious Theodor Eicke, complained that the Volksdeutsche recruits were of poor quality, prone to such cowardly acts as self-inflicting wounds, and lacking ideological fervor.[56] Similar comments were elicited from two commanders of the 1st SS Panzer Division (*Adolf Hitler*), Sepp Dietrich and Fritz Wisch, about the poor quality of the *Volksdeutsche* recruits later in the war.[57]

When a new SS panzer division was created, a few key personnel were transferred from one of the older divisions. When the 12th SS Panzer Division (*Hitler Jugend*) was formed at Beverloo, Belgium in 1943, some of its cadre of officers and NCOs had been transferred from the 1st SS Panzer Division (*Adolf Hitler*). There was still, however, a distinct lack of experience in the division's unit command structure in May 1944. This lack of experience led to grievous losses when the division was committed to battle after the D-Day invasions.[58]

Although the Army was subject to the ever increasing strains on manpower, the best manpower in Germany was allocated to the panzer arm. Down to the end of the war, panzer units did not have to resort to such marks of desperate improvisation as "stomach" or "ear" battalions.[59] Older men and younger boys were employed, however, near the end of the war, with a corresponding decline in combat effectiveness.

Leadership is a rare and valuable commodity in any situation, but it is really at a premium in war. Thus the selection and promotion of officers and NCOs is an extremely important part of developing an army's fighting potential.

During the 1920s General Hans von Seeckt, the head of the *Truppenamt* (the name adopted for the General Staff after it had been outlawed by the Allies), got around the restrictions imposed upon the German Army by the Versailles Treaty by creating a *Führerheer*, or leader army, in which every private, NCO and officer would be able to act in a higher position than his present rank. This required high standards for the selection of men for the Army, and combined with higher pay and better living conditions, made the Army an attractive prospect for many a bright, young and well-educated German volunteer.[60]

High educational standards and a small officer corps allowed for a very methodical selection process for officers, as well as for NCOs. As with so many other personnel questions, selection was usually left in the hands of the regimental commander.[61] The Imperial Army's practice of segregating the promotion tracks of officers and NCOs was also discarded after 1919. Although a difficult process, an NCO could become an officer.[62]

The selection process for SS officers and NCOs was similar to that of the Army, but different in some important ways. Officer candidates and NCOs, like other personnel, were often selected on the basis of racial characteristics, in accordance with Nazi ideology. These would include a minimum height of 5'10", "Aryan" features, and in some cases even perfect teeth.[63]

Promotion was based on a combination of experience and ability. For Army NCOs in peacetime, promotion required at least several years of service in the grade to be obtained. Wartime promotions were considerably faster, but even here promotions to senior NCO grades generally required at least two months in command of a unit in combat.[64] This applied even to such legendary warriors as ace assault gun commander Hugo Primozic, who was promoted to lieutenant only after he spent five months in command of an assault gun platoon, during which time his assault gun destroyed sixty Soviet tanks.[65] The periods required for officer promotions could be longer.

It is also important to point out that German officers and NCOs who were wounded were always returned to their original units.[66] This was in keeping with the importance of having some "old hands" around, and the vital role they played in setting the example for the younger men.[67] Of equal importance was the notion held in the German Army that the presence of an officer to command a unit was not necessary. If no suitable officer could be found, the ranking NCO took over. Under desperate circumstances, such as in Normandy, infantry squads were entrusted to privates who were considered suitable leaders.[68] The guiding principle behind this policy was that a bad officer was considered worse than no officer at all.[69]

German Army personnel policies were designed much more for the combat efficiency than for managerial convenience. In this sense they were very successful. One recent author has contended that the Germans, by concentrating their best manpower in the panzer divisions and other motorized units, really wasted their manpower by relegating the rest of the Army to second class status.[70] This does not hold up under close examination, primarily because of the return the Germans got on their investment in these units. Time and again panzer and motorized divisions intervened to save critical situations. By comparison, the Allies' most expensive investment of manpower, the airborne divisions, were underutilized and fragile in any case, as the battle of Arnhem demonstrated.[71]

Although an excellent fighting force, the panzer arm did suffer from personnel deficiencies. The prime of these was the lack of men who had contact with automotive devices. This, combined with oil and gasoline shortages, heavy use of foreign vehicles and combat losses resulted in shortages of both drivers and maintenance personnel. Here again, the German Army was attuned more to the nineteenth than to the twentieth century.

CHAPTER THREE

Military Training

"Training spares blood!"

—O<small>LD MILITARY MOTTO</small>[1]

"The greatest hindrance in wartime training is the partially uncritically accepted routine of peacetime training."

—G<small>EYR VON</small> S<small>CHWEPPENBURG</small>, 1944[2]

It is only by rigorous training that soldiers can become effective war fighters, at least in peacetime. The length and toughness of training is central to the making of good soldiers and more important, good NCOs and officers. The NCO and officer corps were essential to the strength of the German Army, and that strength reflected the level and intensity of German military training.

During the Nazi era, youths of pre-military age were given rudimentary military training to prepare them for induction into the Army. It should be noted that this was not a new idea. Such a notion had once been proposed by the famous French Socialist Jean Jaures. He had advocated that youths should be given training beginning at the age of thirteen as preparation for military service.[3] While it is unlikely that the Nazis ever read Jaures, they did make use of his idea, or rather carried it to the extreme. For Hitler and Ernst Röhm, a former Army captain who headed the largest Nazi Party organization, the *Sturmabteilung* (SA), the most important thing they could reintroduce to a decadent Germany society was military or "soldierly" virtue.[4] Hence physical fitness and military prowess were central tenets of Nazi ideology. In accordance with this pre-military age youths received what might be described as paramilitary training. This included sports, map reading and terrain exercises. Boys were also taught marksmanship with small caliber rifles.[5]

During the first few years of Nazi rule, all young men from the ages of eighteen to twenty were given military training by the SA. This was reflective of the complex relationship between Hitler, the SA and the Army. Hitler had come to power as the head of a movement that professed to be revolutionary. Although Hitler quickly dropped the revolutionary elements in his rhetoric, the SA and Röhm, this included the SA supplanting the Army as the sole bearer of arms in the nation.[6] Hitler did attempt to mollify the SA in two ways. First, by allowing the SA to conduct military training, and then by authorizing the SA to form a 250,000 man reserve for the Army, which had already exceeded the 100,000 man limit set for it by the Versailles Treaty. These efforts failed, however, and by early 1934 Röhm had gone so far as to call Hitler a "swine."[7] Hitler settled the matter once and for all with the execution of Röhm and his most important followers in the infamous "Night of the Long Knives" purge of 30 June 1934.

The military training conducted by the SA sought to compress the equivalent of American basic training into about four weeks. According to the training plan presented by SA Leader Baldur von Schirach dated 9 October 1933, youths were to be given four weeks of military training, lasting about one hundred and eighty hours. This included marching in formation, and by the twenty-second day a youth was expected to complete a twenty mile march with a twenty-five pound pack. Small-arms training was also given, and there was some limited instruction and training in heavy weapons and tactics.[8]

After the purge of 30 June 1934, the SA was removed from any role in military training, although it retained responsibility for pre- and post-military training as late as 1939.[9] Any military training given to the Hitler Youth was conducted by the Army. For a few months in 1937, the job of liaison with the Hitler

Youth was held by none other than Erwin Rommel. Rommel was most enthusiastic in his association with the Hitler Youth, but clashes with Schirach led to Rommel's removal from the position.[10] By 1937 pre-military training for the Hitler Youth had become more sophisticated. This included special training to be given to youths who were considered particularly suited for service in the Luftwaffe, the Navy, or the motorized troops.[11] There were, naturally, exceptions to this policy.[12]

After passing out of the Hitler Youth, young men went to the National Labor Service (*Reichsarbeitdienst*, or RAD). There they received more paramilitary training, with a heavy emphasis on physical fitness and drill. This kind of training was also designed to inculcate the virtues of group loyalty, cohesion and comradeship, and to prepare them for eventual induction into the armed forces.[13]

Once drafted into the Army proper, a soldier's training would be undertaken by his parent unit. Basic training would be conducted by his division's replacement battalion. The emphasis was on training of a practical nature, with a decided stress on weapons and small unit tactics.[14]

Training was also geared towards achieving a set of basic objectives. These included a high standard of physical fitness, mental preparation for combat, courage to overcome fear, decisiveness, leadership and eagerness for responsibility, to name the most basic qualities that make for soldierly effectiveness.[15] This was accomplished by relatively simple but effective methods such as putting recruits in disorienting or confusing situations to see how they would react. Physical training was designed to push the new recruits to the limits of their endurance.[16]

Once the soldier had completed his basic training with the replacement battalion, he was sent to his parent unit. German training was conducted in accordance with the basic principles espoused by German doctrine. A good example of this is to be found in a U.S. Military Attache report. In February 1937 three U.S. Army officers, Major Truman Smith and

Captains James Crockett and Harland Hartness, spent three days with the 39th Anti-Tank Battalion, part of the 3rd Panzer Division.

The battalion was located in Wunsdorf, the site of the German Army's Tank School, and was a neighboring unit to a battalion of the 8th Panzer Regiment, also part of the 3rd Panzer Division. The units were placed together for training purposes. Although the battalion was considered part of the Panzer Troops, its basic training was the same at that of the infantry. After arriving at the post, soldiers spent the next six months undergoing intense infantry training, with some training on the standard German anti-tank gun of the day, the 37mm. After the initial six month period, the men were broken up into groups. Of these, 45% received specialist training as anti-tank gun crewmen, 40% were trained as vehicle drivers and mechanics and 15% as signalmen. Mixed in with this specialist training were brief resumptions of infantry training.[17]

The pre-war training program included several features that deserve special comment. The first of these is the emphasis on familiarity with combined arms. Tank and anti-tank units were encouraged to train together. The training of troops was only considered complete when each knew and understood completely the functions and capabilities of the other.[18] Also of note here is the fact that all of the battalion's personnel were trained extensively as infantry. This was for two reasons. First, the Germans were constantly aware of the possibility of their having to fight a two-front war in Europe under conditions of numerical inferiority.[19] Under these circumstances, the German Army could not afford to maintain a large number of soldiers who did not serve any kind of combat function. Second, every army is based on infantry, and it is this branch which inevitably absorbs the majority of the casualties. Thus the highest demand will always be for infantrymen, regardless of the army. Also of note in German pre-war training was the amount of training carried out jointly with engineers, as they were considered integral to armor operations as well as anti-tank defense.[20]

This kind of thoroughness also extended to vehicular training and other types of training as well. The German Army ran a Motor Transport Combat School for officers, NCOs and enlisted men. The school was divided into four courses, tactical, technical, firing and motor transport instruction and experimentation. The tactical courses were divided into introductory and training courses. The introductory course was designed to give officers from other branches of the Army a knowledge of the equipment as well as their methods of employment in combat. The training courses gave theoretical and practical training to officers in the motorized branches.

The technical courses were for younger NCOs. They were designed to give them theoretical and practical training in the use and care of vehicles. In order to be admitted to a technical course of any kind, the prospective student had to pass an entrance examination. The NCOs of all motorized units were trained as master mechanics. Firing courses were used to train instructors for tank firing training. Enlisted men who had passed the elementary tests for driver were trained in motor transport instruction and experimentation courses.[21]

It is interesting to contrast this training with that of the U.S. Army. The U.S. Army's approach to basic training was completely different, because it was carried out before a soldier was assigned to a unit. One American Military Attache, Colonel Bernard R. Peyton, argued that this was an advantage because it relieved the soldier's parent unit of the burden.[22] At the unit level, although weapons training was heavily stressed, troops in infantry divisions tended to lack combined arms training, especially integration with tanks.[23] During the August 1941 Louisiana Maneuvers, for example, several soldiers of the U.S. 34th Infantry Division told one historian that they did not see any tanks, at least close up, during maneuvers. One said that he did not see a tank until he got the opportunity to see a German tank in North Africa—after he had been captured.[24] The training of American armored divisions suffered from a variety of equipment shortages and a lack of maintenance and storage facilities for the vehicles.[25]

The German Army used practical training aids, simple but effective devices. In pre-war training, anti-tank troops were given full-scale cardboard silhouettes of armored vehicles taken from Fritz Heigl's popular work, *Taschenbuch der Tanks.*[26] This would not only show troops where and how to aim at targets, but the silhouettes could also be used for a practical course in vehicle identification. Later during the war soldiers were issued tables with which they could learn to estimate ranges.[27] To improve marksmanship, anti-tank troops used a sub-caliber device that allowed them to fire at a moving target that was dragged by a sled.[28] Prospective truck drivers were tested with a simple apparatus consisting of lights, pedals and sounds. The reactions of the subject were recorded and his character and personality were carefully assessed.[29]

It is also worth noting the high standards demanded by the German Army. The goal was to attain both speed and precision. Anti-tank gun crews, for example, were expected to eventually be able to place their gun in firing position and fire "blindfolded."[30] When using the sub-caliber device mentioned previously, known officially as Device 35, a gun crew was expected to be able to fire fifteen rounds in one minute and score seven hits.[31]

The German Army also benefited from the *Anschluss* with Austria and the occupation of Czechoslovakia. The conduct of the mobile units in the *Anschluss,* in this case the 2nd Panzer Division and the SS Regiment *Leibstandarte Adolf Hitler,* revealed serious deficiencies in matters such as vehicle maintenance and march discipline.[32] These were faults that could be rectified by training.

Wartime training was a good deal tougher than peacetime training. The German High Command was disappointed in the performance of their soldiers in the Polish campaign. Halder echoed the complaint made commonly by field commanders that the infantry were not very vigorous in the attack. He also noted that march discipline in the motorized units was poor and resulted in traffic jams.[33] Guderian noted several occasions when his motorized and panzer units exhibited signs of nervousness about going into action.[34]

The Army High Command became well aware of this situation, having been alerted by a number of brutally honest after-action reports from unit commanders disclosing the shortcomings of their troops. The 2nd Light Division, for example, reported that its reconnaissance units failed utterly to produce any kind of results, and instead suffered sharp losses, especially in vehicles.[35] An effort to overcome these deficiencies led to the institution of a stringent training program for both recruits and veterans. Between the Polish and French campaigns there was a concentrated effort to raise the level of efficiency in the Army to a uniformly high level.[36]

The program was intended to raise the level of war-fighting effectiveness as well as to incorporate the lessons of the Polish campaign into the Army's current doctrine. According to the commander of the 10th Panzer Division, Major General Ferdinand Schaal, the goal of the training was to improve the conduct of the troops in combat. They had to be inured to the harshness and stress of combat and the new troops had to be trained in the proper use of combined arms. This included the integration of tanks and infantry, and the use of infiltration tanks by both. Other areas that received attention included march and fuel discipline, as well as reconnaissance.[37] According to the reports filed by the division, that is just what they did, and they did it for months on end.[38]

Like their Army counterparts, SS units also went through the same program. During the period between the Polish and French campaigns, Eicke's SS *Totenkopf* Division went through a rigorous training program, designed to fully acquaint junior officers and NCOs with tactics in several kinds of fighting, including that in urban and heavily forested areas. Individual soldiers practiced marksmanship, while units conducted exercises in river crossing and night fighting. The SS *Leibstandarte Adolf Hitler*, expanded to brigade strength between the Polish and French campaigns, went through a similar training program.[39] This kind of training was designed to test the very limits of endurance of both officers and men. In doing so it eliminated those who were unfit for combat, while those who were fit were honed to a very fine edge by May 1940.[40]

As in so many other areas, there was a clear connection between the German Army of World War II and its Imperial predecessor. Often live ammunition was used in training exercises, a practice employed by the pre-1914 Imperial German Army during some phases of their annual summer maneuvers. Although casualties did occur occasionally, as a German officer explained to American Military Attache Lieutenant Colonel W. D. Hohenthal, the practice put the men on alert to become more effective in combat.[41] As late as 7 May 1940, a mere three days before the start of operations in the west, SS units were still conducting these kinds of exercises.[42] Units also conducted training with live ammunition during their rest, refitting or rebuilding periods.[43]

The Germans retained this kind of realistic training for the duration of the war. Before undertaking the Balkan campaign in 1941, the 11th Panzer Division spent the winter training for operations in "impassable" mountains.[44] This paid fine dividends, both tactically and strategically, in the subsequent campaign. During the autumn of 1940, as part of the preparation for the invasion of the Soviet Union, OKH ordered another round of intense training. Panzer divisions were to train extensively in combined arms tactics, especially in the integration of tanks, infantry and artillery in either massed tank attacks or in mixed battle groups. Motorized infantry divisions were to train for fighting unsupported and to clear forests and villages quickly.[45] In North Africa before the opening of the Gazala offensive in the spring of 1942, the 21st Panzer Division conducted extensive combined arms training, especially in the use of infiltration attacks by infantry.[46]

Another area the Germans paid a great deal of attention to after their initial experiences was night combat training. During the Polish and French campaigns there was little in the way of night combat.[47] The 1941 campaign in the Soviet

Union, however, gave the Germans a nasty shock. The Russians excelled in night combat, and night patrols, ambushes and skirmishes were terrifying to German soldiers.[48] The various branches of the Army quickly took this in hand. Thereafter, German training documents laid great stress on night combat training for all branches.[49]

The Germans always took great pains to make sure that the combat lessons learned from the latest campaign were quickly incorporated into training. On 4 October 1940, for example, American Military Attache Lieutenant Colonel W. D. Hohenthal visited the German Army's Tank School at Wunsdorf. The commandant, Major General Josef Harpe, explained that all the instructors were combat veterans who had just fought in the French campaign. In keeping with normal German Army training, independence and self-sufficiency were stressed. In terrain appreciation, for example, commanders were expected to know the terrain they were operating in so well that they would not need maps. Repeated reference to maps was considered a sign that the leadership was either lacking in confidence or poorly trained.[50]

The Tank School at Wunsdorf retained its importance for training throughout the war. It would issue short instructions for training, especially for junior officers.[51] Units themselves incorporated the lessons compiled from after-action reports into their own training schedules. Just over a month before Kursk, the *Gross Deutschland* Panzer Grenadier Division issued a short three page piece for its subordinate commanders on the organization, command and training of panzer grenadiers.[52] Prior to Normandy, General Geyr von Schweppenburg, commander of Panzer Group West, issued a series of training directives. The fourth of these laid out the prescription for what constituted good training. The best combat training, according to Geyr, was based on a combination of combat experience and "soldier sense," supported by the latest bulletins and after-action reports.[53] Later on, before its commitment to the Normandy front, the 116th Panzer Division consolidated the contents of a number of after-action reports filed by divisions already fighting there into a short circular that could be distributed to the division's subordinate units.[54]

One area the Germans paid attention to early on was cooperation between air power and ground units. Luftwaffe General Walter Wever was instrumental in the developing of air liaison officers (*Flieger Verbindungs Offiziere*, or *Flivos*) to facilitate communication between air and ground units. In addition, both Army and Luftwaffe officers were trained to understand the other service's operational doctrine. These were vital first steps in the development of a common close air support doctrine for both the Army and the Luftwaffe.[55]

The Spanish Civil War provided valuable experience in cooperation between the Luftwaffe's Condor Legion and German ground units operating in Spain. The Germans were also fortunate to have Luftwaffe General Wolfram von Richthofen in Spain, a true visionary in the area of close air support.[56] Thus, when the German Army invaded Poland on 1 September 1939, of all the armies in Europe, only it had a practical, if flawed, doctrine of close air support of army units by the Luftwaffe.

Experiences in Poland, however, uncovered the problems involved in the support of ground units by aircraft, especially in fluid situations. The 4th Light Division, for example, was attacked three times on each of three days (a total of nine) by Germany aircraft.[57] These kinds of problems persisted during the French campaign. Dissatisfied with air-ground cooperation during the Polish and French campaigns, the Army High Command directed all higher headquarters to conduct cooperative training with the Luftwaffe every time a favorable moment presented itself.[58] This type of training was aided by the fact that both the Army and the Luftwaffe were completely committed to the kind of cooperation required to make it work in both training and operations.[59] This kind of training continued for the duration of the war, so long as the Luftwaffe possessed the sufficient strength for undertaking such missions. During the lull before the battle of Kursk, for example, the 2nd SS Panzer Grenadier Division (*Das Reich*) conducted intense training, culminating in a division-sized assault exercise with Stuka dive bombers in support.[60]

In terms of the way training affected the individual soldier, perhaps the best description we have is to be found in Guy Sajer's historical novel, *The Forgotten Soldier*. Sajer's novel is about an Alsatian who is conscripted into the German Army in 1942. Eventually he volunteers for and spends the rest of the war with the Army's elite *Gross Deutschland* Panzer Division as an infantryman.[61]

Sajer's depiction of the training camp run by the division's field replacement battalion in 1943 before joining his company is starkly realistic. It is complete with training methods that exposed soldiers to serious injuries, and even resulted in some deaths.[62] The accuracy of Sajer's depictions is confirmed by examining the training regimen of the SS Panzer Grenadier School, established at Benneschau in Bohemia in the summer of 1942, and subsequently opened in January 1943. Some of the training methods included having soldiers dig foxholes and cower in them while tanks were driven over them. Some additional practices included having soldiers lie prone on open ground between two moving tanks, jumping on a moving tank to place a magnetic mine on the side of the turret, and disabling a tank with a demolition charge. The purpose of this was to diminish a soldier's fear of tanks.[63] It was also vital to the eventual training of individual soldiers in the proficient use of short-range hand-fired anti-tank weapons used by the Germans in the later stages of the war.[64] The Germans certainly believed that this kind of training was essential for preparing men for combat. The I SS Panzer Corps adopted an old training motto from the pre-1914 French Army, "training spares blood."[65]

The training of officers and NCOs, as noted before, was both long and thorough. In the *Reichswehr*, training courses were long since both officers and NCOs were trained to act in a capacity two steps above their rank.[66] This proved a valuable asset in the Army's rapid expansion after 1935. Training school programs for officers and NCOs were very demanding, and as a result there was a high drop out rate. This, however, was not necessarily a drawback, because the washouts took their training experience back to their units and it made them better soldiers. This was true of the SS as well.[67]

Training for the SS was at once both similar to and different from that of the Army. Since the Army held the "high ground," the SS was initially dependent on the Army for training areas and instruction in the use of weapons. Between 1934 and 1944, the SS established four officers candidate schools (*Junkerschulen*) at Bad Tolz (1934), Braunschweig (1935), Klagenfurt (1943), and Prague (1944).[68] Along with these, the SS also had a number of branch schools, the most important of which was the SS Panzer Grenadier School, established in 1942 at Benneschau, in Bohemia.[69]

All of these schools, however, were generally run along Army lines. The similarities included the length of the course and training schedule that was followed.[70] The only major difference lay in the degree of ideological training given to SS officer candidates, which included the study of such Nazi "classics" as *Mein Kampf*, Alfred Rosenberg's *The Myth of the Twentieth Century* and Walter Darre's *Blood and Soil*. This was also done in SS divisions on a unit basis.[71] While Army soldiers did not have the same degree of organized ideological training as the SS, soldiers were certainly encouraged to read, and did read, such popular Nazi publications as *Der Stürmer*.[72] To insure uniformity of military training, SS schools used Army manuals. In addition, from 1935 on, SS officers could be trained at Army schools and then returned to their original units.[73]

These schools were of critical importance to the SS in enabling it to expand successfully during the war. From 1934 until the outbreak of war a total of nine classes were graduated from the *Junkerschulen*, each requiring ten months to complete the school's program.[74] Since the schools before the war could produce up to five hundred officers annually, and very few of these were required for military service initially, there was a large reserve of officers available to staff divisions after 1940. During the war, the SS Junkerschulen furnished the SS with about 15,000 trained officers.[75]

From the point of view of the panzer arm, there are several significant points to observe with respect to German Army training. First is the great weight attached to the Army's basic doctrine in its relation to training, especially the principle of combined arms. In the Imperial German Army, officers attending the *Kriegsakademie* spent the late summer and early fall months going through cross-branch training, so that officers could become acquainted with all of the Army's arms and their capabilities.[76] In the German Army of World War II, German soldiers, NCOs and officers were all trained to understand the value of the combination of tanks, infantry, artillery and engineers. This not only allowed individual divisions to employ combined arms battle groups (*Kampfgruppen*), but also allowed panzer divisions to do this in concert with non-motorized infantry divisions. This doctrine and its practice had been stressed as the basic German armor doctrine before the war.[77]

This was reinforced by the kind of cross-branch training courses similar to those of the Imperial Army. In February 1940, the OKH Training Section set up a series of three-week courses to give staff officers cross-branch training. Officers were to be drawn from all divisions, including SS.[78] Equally important, this was the accepted doctrine of the German Army as a whole. During the later stage of the war Guderian, in his capacity as Inspector General of Panzer Troops, passed binding instructions on the Replacement Army for training every type of soldier to cope with armored warfare. Such instructions were instrumental in maintaining uniformity of training.[79] This gave the German Army a tremendous edge over the U.S. Army, which lacked not only combined arms training, but did not even have a combined arms doctrine that all the major branches could agree on.[80]

Second, the raising of so many divisions and their occasional rotation out of the line allowed them valuable time for training as well as refitting.[81] Rotation made possible the incorporation of trained replacements and kept a sharp combat edge on divisions. In addition, the German policy of giving everybody combat training made the necessary rear area "comb outs" a relatively successful means of keeping combat units up to strength, at least temporarily. German personnel policy was an important factor here as well. German divisions were not subject to the "personnel raids" that proved so disruptive to many American divisions during their training cycles. One American division, for example, lost a cumulative total of 22,235 men to the Army Ground Forces as replacements, the result of which was to reduce its training efforts to a shambles.[82]

Finally, there was the emphasis on individual as well as command initiative and flexibility. This had its roots in the Imperial Army's infantry regulations of 1888, written largely by General Sigismund von Schlichting.[83] This was then carried on in the form of the development of infiltration tactics developed by the German Army during World War I.[84] One element of pre-1939 German military training that American military attaches found noteworthy was that the German Army lacked a "school solution" to solve problems.[85] Soldiers, NCOs and officers were trained to judge each situation as being unique and not to react in a dogmatic fashion. This attitude was reflected throughout German manuals, beginning with the basic German field service regulation, *Truppenführung*, with its Clausewitzian definition of war as an "art, depending upon free creative activity, scientifically grounded."[86]

Wartime training stressed the chaotic nature of combat and its effect on command. Here there was a bit of division in how the armor and infantry parts of the panzer arm approached this. Panzer grenadier unit commanders, especially at the company and platoon levels, were cautioned as to the impossibility of issuing "methodical" orders once an attack started. Once that was the case, the best thing they could do was to set a good example for their men in combat.[87] Tank company commanders, on the other hand, were told that they were to both command and fight, but command was the most important of their functions.[88]

The declining fortunes of war exercised a deleterious effect on training. This was primarily manifested in reduced time for training courses. Panzer troops received twenty-one weeks of training during the early part of the war. By 1944 this had been reduced to sixteen weeks.[89] The SS Junkerschulen were forced to reduce the length of their training courses from ten months to four.[90] Training was also undoubtedly hindered by shortages of equipment and more importantly fuel.[91]

These circumstances ultimately caught the Germans in a vicious circle. Less well-trained men were more liable to become casualties. Higher casualties in turn generated a greater demand for replacements. The losses in infantry in panzer and panzer grenadier divisions in turn generated losses of other kinds. To fill gaps in infantry units, men "combed out" of artillery and flak units were often sent into the line.[92] In addition, the division's reconnaissance and engineer battalions were often committed to hold part of the line. While the engineers could certainly do the job, given the "make do" approach of the German Army, it deprived the commander of an important asset with special capabilities.[93] The nature of combat operations late in the war also contributed to the problem of the loss of soldiers with specialized training. In Normandy, Allied air superiority largely confined the Germans to moving at night. This led to an increase in vehicular accidents, and a corresponding increase in the loss of drivers.[94]

The Germans did attempt to partially remedy this by having higher echelon units set up their own schools to make up for the limited time available at established schools. This began as early as late 1942, when a school for field NCOs in the mobile troops was established at Rembertow, near Warsaw in Poland. Units were expected to send men there for training, even during the climax of the abortive attempt to rescue the trapped German Sixth Army at Stalingrad.[95] During the autumn of 1944, Army Group B set up its own informal schools to give junior officers and NCOs more training. Schools were set up at the division, corps and army levels. They were located at sites that were close to their parent units, and the courses were designed to last about eight days.[96] Measures such as these, however successful, could not rescue the

German Army from the consequences of the casualties they were suffering on all fronts.

In conclusion, it is clearly evident that German Army training reflected to a very great degree the most basic German Army doctrine of individual, small unit, and divisional initiative. This played an extremely important part in allowing the Germans to employ their divisions as they did and maintain a relatively high standard of leadership at the company and field grade levels throughout the war. It is also important to note that, at least in the training of infantry, the German Army still adhered to the concepts developed in the late stages of World War I. This can be seen clearly in not only the ideas espoused in the manuals, but even in the language in which these ideas were presented.[97] Here again there is a clear continuity between the German Army of World War II and its imperial predecessor.

Pz.Kpfw.III Ausf.L from 16. Infanterie-Division (mot) in Woronesch on July 22, 1942.

Pz.Kpfw.IV Ausf.H in Italy in 1944.

Sturmgeschütz III Ausf.B from Sturmgeschütz-Abteilung 192.

Pz.Kpfw.I Ausf.A.

Same Pz.Kpfw.I Ausf.A as the bottom photo on the previous page, with its machine guns removed.

Pz.Kpfw.IIs with French prisoners of war.

Destroyed Pz.Kpfw.Panther Ausf.A on the Western Front.

Pz.Kpfw.III Ausf.G.

An interesting photograph showing a Pz.Kpfw.III Ausf.E or F converted to Tauchpanzer, and which appears to have the outer half of its 37mm gun removed.

Pz.Kpfw.III Ausf.B.

Pz.Kpfw.III Ausf.N from s.Pz.Abt.501 in Tunisia on March 11, 1943.

Destroyed Tiger II, less one gun, in Belgium.

Jagdpanther destroyed by the US 10th Tank Battalion on April 9, 1945, at the outskirts of Equord, Germany. As can be seen, the frontal armor was quite resilient, having resisted at least five impacts.

Pz.Kpfw.IV Ausf.D with bolted-on 30mm armor plates.

A Nashorn, with the vehicle name "Tiger", on the Eastern Front on March 13, 1944.

Hummel.

Destroyed Panzerjäger I.

Pz.Kpfw.III Ausf.B.

Destroyed Pz.Kpfw.Panther Ausf.A on the Western Front.

Tiger I from 3./s.Pz.Abt.502 on the Eastern Front in August 1943.

Destroyed Sturmgeschütz III Ausf.G and Kübelwagen on the Western Front.

Destroyed Pz.Kpfw.Panther Ausf.A on the Western Front. The impact damage can be clearly seen on the front left corner.

Destroyed Tiger I in a French village. The two U.S. soldiers are inspecting the impact holes, not visible from this angle, which disabled the tank.

Tiger I.

Pz.Kpfw.IVs in Greece, receiving critique after an exercise, July 1, 1943.

Pz.Kpfw.38(t).

Pz.Kpfw.35(t).

CHAPTER FOUR

Doctrine: Correcting the Myths[1]

"It was principally the books and articles of the Englishmen, Fuller, Liddell-Hart and Martel that excited my interest and gave me food for thought."
—HEINZ GUDERIAN, 1952[2]

"We consider the situation to be like that of 1918, as the then OHL allowed the cavalry to be dismounted, confined to the trenches and thus deprived of the prospects of a great victory, since turning the great spring offensive into a permanent breakthrough required better use of mobile units. . . . To return to our characteristic conduct of war, we need an operational reserve."
—HEINZ GUDERIAN, 23 MARCH 1944[3]

If there has been any military organization subject to myth-making, it is the German Army of World War II. This is particularly true when it comes to the matter of armor doctrine, and its corollary, anti-tank doctrine, which is still clouded with myths and distortions. These myths center around several issues in particular. First, what were the sources of German armor and anti-tank doctrine? The answer to this question must address the notion of foreign (especially British) influence on German doctrine. Did the Germans read the works of B. H. Liddell-Hart, J.F.C. Fuller and Charles de Gaulle, and more important, did their writings have an effect on German doctrine? An examination of German armor doctrine must also deal with some very broad questions. Was German armor doctrine representative of the German Army's approach to war in general? Was it truly innovative, as the term Blitzkrieg implies, or was it something else? The answers to these questions will provide us with as clear a picture as possible of German doctrine and tell us something about the nature of the German Army as well.

The notion of British influence on German doctrine really rests on two paragraphs in the English edition of Heinz Guderian's memoir, *Panzer Leader*. Though quoted many times, the passage is worth repeating here:

> It was principally the books and articles of the Englishmen, Fuller, Liddell-Hart and Martel, that excited my interest and gave me food for thought. These far-sighted soldiers were even then trying to make the tank more than just an infantry support weapon. They envisaged it in relationship to the growing motorization of our age, and thus they became pioneers of a new type of warfare on the largest scale.
>
> I learned from them the concentration of armor, as employed in the battle of Cambrai. Furthermore, it was Liddell-Hart who emphasized the use of armored forces for long-range strokes, operations against the opposing army's communications, and also proposed a type of armored division combining panzer and panzer-infantry units. Deeply impressed by these ideas I tried to develop them in a sense practicable for our own army. So I owe many suggestions of our further development to Captain Liddell-Hart.[4]

This passage has been taken at face value and uncritically accepted by many popular writers and even by some scholars of the subjects.[5] A good deal of the passage previously quoted, however, can be dismissed as material written specifically for the post-war British public, or perhaps an appeal to Liddell-Hart's vanity.[6] Guderian's English biographer, Kenneth Macksey, noted that the second paragraph of the passage is not in the original German edition of Guderian's memoir.[7] One German writer has asserted that Guderian only became aware of Liddell-Hart's writings after the war, when they corresponded.[8]

Were the Germans aware of the works of the foreign theorists? The answer to that was undoubtedly yes. Foreign developments in tanks were monitored and reported on in the pages of the standard German military periodical, *Militär Wochenblatt.* These consisted of brief pieces by known writers, or by military attaches posted to foreign countries, along with brief unsigned summaries of foreign works.[9]

A more obvious way of examining this question would be to see which authors were cited in footnotes or listed in the bibliographies of German works. Using this method, it is clear that the Germans were much more familiar with the works of Fuller and de Gaulle than those of Liddell-Hart. Guderian, for example, mentioned Liddell-Hart only once in his pre-war writing.[10] His most important pre-war article, "Die Panzertruppen und ihr Zusammenwirken mit den anderen Waffen," published in the August 1936 edition of *Militärwissenschaftliche Rundschau,* quotes both Fuller and de Gaulle, but not Liddell-Hart.[11] The same is true of the bibliography of *Achtung-Panzer!*[12] In other documents and writings as well, it is Fuller's name that appears, not Liddell-Hart's.[13]

It would seem then, that the influence exerted by these theorists on German doctrinal development was minimal at best. While the works of Fuller, de Gaulle and to a much lesser extent Liddell-Hart were read, they were certainly not considered an essential part of an officer's military education. An American Military Attaché report dated 3 December 1940 gave an officially prescribed list of works for officers to read. The list was broken down into several sections. The general section included Carl von Clausewitz, Alfred von Schlieffen and Waldemar Erfurth. The historical section included the German official history of World War I, *Die Weltkrieg,* as well as the memoirs of Hans von Seeckt, Paul von Hindenburg, Erich Ludendorff, Conrad von Hötzendorf and August von Mackensen. The technical section contained works on armor, including Guderian's *Achtung-Panzer!* and Walter Nehring's *Panzerabwehr.* The entire list, however, contained not a single work by a foreign theorist.[14]

If foreign influence is discounted, the question still remains: What were the sources of German armor and anti-tank doctrine? German interest in tanks originated from several sources. First, it was perfectly natural that the German Army should be interested in tanks. They had been on the receiving end of several devastating tank attacks during World War I, the most notable being at Amiens, where some four hundred British tanks completely overwhelmed the German defenses in a rout.[15] The German Army also developed a tank force of its own in World War I. It was pitifully small, however, in comparison with its British counterpart, consisting of only ninety tanks by the summer of 1918.[16] The Germans had more extensive experience with wheeled motor vehicles. In 1914 the German advance into Belgium was sustained logistically in part by the use of confiscated Belgian trucks to supplement their own motor transport.[17] Later in the war, the Germans experimented with motorized combat forces. General Erich von Falkenhayn used column of truck-borne infantry with great success in the conquest of Romania.[18] Finally, the restrictions imposed on the Germans by the Versailles Treaty caused them to think about how to defend against tanks when they were allowed none themselves.

German interest in tanks continued during the 1920s. The Reichswehr had information on tanks collected during the 1920s.[19] The Chief of the General Staff, General Hans von Seeckt, though he had no practical experience with tanks in either a theoretical or practical sense, was nonetheless a strong supporter of tank development. He ordered that all units conduct theoretical training in armored warfare using mockups of known French or British tanks.[20] The use of dummy tanks became a standard feature of German Army maneuvers. This practice earned very favorable comments from the American Military Attaché.[21]

Aside from those activities that could be legally undertaken within the constraints imposed by the Versailles Treaty, the Germans conducted tank testing and training at the secret joint Russo-German tank school at Kazan in the Soviet Union from 1929 to 1933. Although considerably smaller than the Russo-German flying school at Lipetsk, and marked by not a little distrust between the Germans and the Soviets, it was still very important from the German point of view. It provided the Germans with some practical experience in working with tanks that was unavailable in Germany. It is worth noting that some of the German Army's leading thinkers on and practitioners of armored warfare and anti-tank defense, such as Ernst Volck-heim, Walter Nehring, and Hans-Georg Reinhardt, were all graduates of the tank school at Kazan.[22]

German armor doctrine as it finally evolved was essentially an outgrowth of the Army's infiltration tactics that it had developed during World War I. These tactics represented a philosophical approach by the German Army intended to break the deadlock of trench warfare. They were based on the use of small groups of specially trained assault infantry using combined arms; in this case, a mix of rifles, light machine guns, grenades and mortars.[23] These groups, after a brief but intense artillery using large amounts of gas and smoke shells, were to penetrate the soft spots in the enemy line and then move into the enemy's rear area. Isolated and bypassed enemy strongpoints would then be assaulted and taken by units following up after the initial advance. These tactics had proven very effective in Russia, Romania, Italy and finally France.[24]

Although Germany ultimately lost World War I, the Germans, and Seeckt in particular, believed that they had developed the correct tactical and operational concepts. The 1921 field service regulation, *Führung und Gefecht*, advocated the use of speed and mobility. The principle of combined arms was heavily emphasized, especially in a deliberate attack.[25] *Führung und Gefecht* also noted the possibility of using trucks to carry infantry and machine gun platoons in conducting a pursuit.[26]

Consistent with these ideas, Seeckt gave high priority to motorizing the artillery for support. Armored cars would take the place of tanks in providing armored support.[27] These ideas were also discussed in various German military publications at the same time.[28] Thus, the basic elements of German armor doctrine were present well before the emergence of the panzer arm.

The principles of anti-tank defense in Germany also date from the 1920s. Here the Germans may have gained from the Versailles Treaty, which prohibited them from having tanks. The most basic principle of anti-tank defense is that the best defense against a tank is another tank. This notion was advocated by thinkers such as J.F.C. Fuller and Fritz Heigl.[29] Since the German Army was denied this means of defense by the treaty, a different means of dealing with the tank had to be found. The 1921 regulations had advocated a system using anti-tank rifles, heavy weapons, guns and flame throwers.[30] Later, Lieutenant Uto Gallwitz argued that anti-tank defense should be based on the gun, used in combination with the machine gun.[31] Batteries of anti-tank guns were to be deployed in "nests," supported by platoons of machine guns. These nests were to be mutually supporting and deployed in depth.[32] Ernst Volckheim also advocated the use of the towed anti-tank gun as the principal means of anti-tank defense, aided by the use of machine guns firing armor-piercing bullets, mines and obstacles.[33]

These influences made German armor doctrine quite different in a number of ways from that propounded by the British theorists. The most important of these differences was the emphasis on combined arms. As noted previously, this had been an important tenet behind the German infiltration tactics of World War I, and the Germans fitted tanks into this concept. In August of 1935 the Germans held their first field maneuver with a panzer division commanded by General Oswald Lutz who, although depicted by Guderian as nothing more than his superior and protector, was also a fine armor theorist in his own right.[34] The after-action report on the exercise, signed by Lutz, stated quite clearly that infantry and tanks must work very closely together.[35] This was in direct contravention to many of the writings of Fuller and Liddell-Hart. Fuller, for example, stated as late as 1932 that infantry would be useful only in places that were inaccessible to tanks.[36] As for Liddell-Hart, while his views were somewhat more sophisticated than those of Fuller, they were marred by Liddell-Hart's rather poor use of analogy. In *Paris or the Future of War*, Liddell-Hart envisioned tanks as the "modern form of heavy cavalry," which would be used against communications and headquarters, a function never performed by heavy cavalry.[37] He repeated this in *The Remaking of Modern Armies*, and then went on to say that "the tank assault of tomorrow is but the long-awaited rebirth of the cavalry charge," a statement that proved to be an accurate description of so many unsupported British tank attacks in North Africa and Normandy, shot to pieces by combined arms German defenses.[38]

Another important element of German combined arms doctrine was the use of engineers. This was advocated as early as 1935 in the first after-action report written on the exercises of the first German panzer division.[39] Later on, Guderian and other writers dwelt on the importance of engineers and found the ultimate reflection of this in the 1938 manual *Richtlinien für die Führung der Panzerdivision*.[40] Engineers became an important element in operations throughout the war. Their special capabilities, such as bridging water obstacles, removing obstructions from roads, the laying and clearing of mines and their ability to attack fortified positions were vital to the progress of panzer operations. They were also able to fight as regular infantry, which was reflective of the German Army's ability to "make do" with any kind of troops in various circumstances.[41] This was also reflective of the German Army's tradition of avoiding the creation of corps of specialist engineer troops, a practice that dated back to Frederick the Great.[42]

The use of air power was also relevant to the development of doctrine. Both Fuller and Liddell-Hart made nothing more than some nebulous statements in this area, forecasting aircraft in the role of "flying artillery."[43] The Germans, however, saw aircraft as a versatile weapon. During the 1920s Captain Helmut Wilberg, Chief of the *Truppenamt's* Air Organization Section, developed a Reichswehr air doctrine that envisioned aircraft being employed in a variety of roles.[44] These included air superiority, interdiction, and strategic as well as tactical bombing. Close air support was not a top priority, owing to the difficulties in communications between ground troops and aircraft.

German Army officers often argued that aircraft were more useful for interdiction than serving as flying artillery. In his classic work on defense, Field Marshal Wilhelm Ritter von Leeb wrote that when on the defensive, air power was important for disrupting the enemy's rear.[45] Guderian argued that air power could facilitate an armored assault by attacks on enemy communications, headquarters and assembly areas, aside from front line positions.[46] But it was also argued as late as 1934 that the utilization of air power for ground attack was impractical. This line of reasoning held that ground attack operations could be conducted only if complete command of the air was attained, something that was not thought possible.[47]

The Germans, however, did take steps towards effecting air-ground cooperation, through the untiring efforts of Luftwaffe Generals Wolfram von Richthofen and Hugo Sperrle, as well as through valuable experience gained in the Spanish Civil War.[48] Nevertheless, the sections of the 1938 manual *Richtlinien für die Führung der Panzerdivision* dealing with artillery make it quite clear that the Army did not expect immediate cooperation from the Luftwaffe in a tactical sense. Panzer division commanders, for example, were advised to have artillery elements in march columns well forward in the group, allowing them to deploy and open fire as soon as possible.[49] Clearly implied here was the notion that aircraft would not be available to directly support ground troops in any immediate sense, thus the emphasis on having the artillery forward. This was reinforced in the manual's section on attack. In most attack scenarios, panzer division commanders were told they would have to do without air support.[50]

German armor and anti-tank doctrine was the product of a vibrant intellectual atmosphere. After 1945, the role of armored warfare guru was appropriated by Heinz Guderian, with the publication of the English language edition of his memoir, *Panzer Leader*, in 1952. In it, Guderian portrays himself as the sole progenitor of German armor doctrine. Men such as Lutz and Erich von Tschischwitz simply fulfill roles as Guderian's patrons, and Fritz Heigl, who was one of Germany's first thinkers on tanks, was reduced to the status of being an "upright German gentleman."[51] This picture gained a great deal of currency in the English speaking world, and even in Germany.[52]

In fact, there were a number of writers who were pondering these matters in Germany throughout the inter-war period. Writers such as Fritz Heigl and Ernst Volckheim were publishing works on tanks and their uses long before Guderian made his mark as an armor theorist. Volckheim was a veteran of the small German tank corps of World War I, when he commanded a German A7V tank. Later he attended the tank school at Kazan and was responsible for writing a number of manuals concerning tank units in the 1930s.[53] A prolific writer, Volckheim advocated the use of combined arms and that a tank force employ several types of tanks to fill several roles, including operations against fortified positions and in pursuit.[54]

A good deal of thought was also given to tank defense as well. Lieutenant Colonel (later General) Walter Nehring was one of the great progenitors of anti-tank doctrine, proposing a very sophisticated approach to the problem, involving a wide array of weapons, including anti-tank guns, tanks, artillery, aircraft and heavy weapons.[55] Austrian General Ludwig Ritter von Eimannsberger was a prolific writer who enjoyed a wide audience in Germany. In 1938 he advanced the idea that anti-aircraft guns firing armor-piercing rounds would be useful in anti-tank defense.[56] These ideas on antitank defense enjoyed wide acceptance among German writers. Guderian, for example, when he did deal with anti-tank defense, relied heavily on Nehring's ideas, as did other writers.[57]

A survey of German military and periodical literature makes it quite clear that while Guderian was an important theorist, he was by no means singular in this regard. The best example of this can be seen after the French campaign. Following the conclusion of the French campaign, it was decided to revise the manual *Richtlinien für die Führung der Panzerdivision*, which had been issued in 1938, to incorporate the lessons learned in the Polish and French campaigns. If Guderian's position as an armor theorist was as preeminent as he made it out to be, one would have expected that he would have been assigned this task. Instead, General Rudolf Schmidt, commander of the XXXIX Army Corps, was given the job. General Franz Halder, Chief of the General Staff, sent Guderian a message on 10 October 1940, simply requesting him to give his opinion on Schmidt's revisions, and to give them in only eight days time at that.[58]

Another false notion disseminated by Guderian in his memoir concerns the character of General Ludwig Beck, Chief of the General Staff from 1933 to 1938. In *Panzer Leader*, Guderian painted Beck as a reactionary who fought against the acceptance of panzer divisions in the German Army.[59] A look at the manuals prepared under Beck and simultaneous developments in the Army shows that Guderian's image of Beck was incorrect at best, mendacious at worst. An obvious development to prove this was that, as noted by Beck's biographer Klaus-Jürgen Müller, the number of panzer divisions in the Army was raised to a total of six.[60] Beck also aided the development of the panzer arm by devoting scarce resources to experimentation with and development of tanks, by no means a certain investment in the early to mid 1930s.[61] Like Seeckt, Beck preferred to have a small, but completely motorized force. His designs were frustrated, however, by the breakneck pace of Hitler's military expansion and by Germany's inability to produce the requisite numbers of vehicles, not to mention the amount of fuel needed.[62]

Perhaps the two most important manuals issued by the German Army during Beck's tenure as Chief of the General Staff were *Truppenführung*, issued in 1933, and *Richtlinien für die Führung der Panzerdivision*, issued in 1938. *Truppenführung* was in effect the successor to *Führung und Gefecht*. If one examines the two manuals, one can see a clear continuity of thinking between Seeckt and Beck. Both manuals emphasized the principles of mobility and combined arms. Another important element stressed was that of individual initiative, especially on the part of junior officers and NCOs. This was clearly expressed in *Führung und Gefecht* and perhaps more famously in *Truppenführung*, where war was defined in the best tradition of Clausewitz as a "free creative activity."[63]

This notion was in part an outgrowth of German infiltration tactics, which demanded a great deal of initiative on the part of junior officers and NCOs, who now became "key decision makers."[64] The very origins of the concept date back in Germany to the nineteenth century. Helmuth von Moltke himself was both a believer in and a practitioner of the principle of giving subordinate commanders a wide degree of latitude, especially at corps and division levels.[65] This was extended downward to field and company grade commanders in 1888 by the infantry regulations written by Prussian General Sigismund von Schlichting.[66] During World War I these concepts were developed and refined into the "infiltration tactics" used by the German Army with success in the later stages of World War I.

A fine example of someone employing these tactics was Erwin Rommel. During World War I, he commanded troops trained in these tactics in Italy. Although only a captain, he occasionally commanded units up to battalion strength. In all of these operations he really had to rely on his own initiative and judgement.[67] These ideas remained a staple of general German doctrine throughout World War II.

The ideas enunciated in *Truppenführung* can also be clearly seen in the manuals that set down German armored doctrine. The concept of combined arms was expressed in *Richtlinien für die Führung der Panzerdivision* by the notion of breaking the division down into combined arms battle groups, or *Kampfgruppen.*[68] This system was used in Poland with what the Germans felt were satisfactory results. Although the conduct of the troops was criticized, and there were calls for improvements in combat techniques, after-action reports stated that the doctrinal principles proved correct.[69] The German Army fought by these ideas throughout the war.

Another important element of German doctrine that was an outgrowth of the German Army's concept of war was the absence of a "school solution." This idea comes through very clearly in both articles and manuals. In his first article, "Truppen auf Kraftwagen und Fliegerabwehr," Guderian, in writing on the subject of air defense for motorized units, stated "binding regulations should not be given for all cases."[70] The basic training manual for tank units, *Vorläufige Anweisungen für die Ausbildung von Panzereinheiten,* given essentially the same advice as to the authority of the commander on the spot.[71] American military attaches were very impressed by the idea and how German military training instructed officers and NCOs to realize that there could be several solutions to a problem. The concept of a "school solution" was eschewed as being entirely too rigid and dogmatic.[72] This looseness in German doctrine led one noted panzer commander, General Leo Freiherr Geyr von Schweppenburg, to make the extravagant claim after the war that there was no such thing as an overall German panzer doctrine.[73]

The Germans were also very successful in being able to alter and refine elements of their doctrine. Although the Germans were well ahead of everyone in terms of air-ground cooperation, Army cooperation with the Luftwaffe had not always been very successful in Poland and France. In the Polish campaign, for example, the 4th Light Division had the unfortunate experience of being mistakenly bombed by the Luftwaffe a number of times.[74] The 10th Panzer Division's after-action report on the Polish campaign went so far as to recommend that part of the Luftwaffe be subordinated to the Army.[75] The 6th Panzer Division noted that cooperation with the Luftwaffe in the French campaign was still not entirely satisfactory.[76] The kind of attitude on the part of the Army as exemplified in the 10th Panzer Division report cited above prompted a response from Richthofen. He admonished that the Luftwaffe was not the Army's "whore."[77] There were other situations, however, where air power was used with great success, especially in the crossing of the Meuse River. The experience of the Polish and French campaigns were duly noted and incorporated into the 1940 manual *Richtlinien für Führung und Einsatz der Panzer-Division*. This manual stated quite definitely how valuable air power could be in facilitating the division's operations.[78]

Equally interesting was the absorbing by the Germans from the Polish and French campaigns of the psychological value of the panzer division. During these early campaigns enemy soldiers, especially low-grade French units, were demoralized by the mere sight of large numbers of tanks.[79] The psychological aspect was stressed in the opening section of the 1940 manual.[80]

Many elements of German pre-war doctrine endured throughout the war. The concept of combined arms has already been noted. Ideas on anti-tank defense also remained essentially the same. During the 1920s some German writers such as Heigl stated that ideally, the best defense against a tank was another tank.[81] The gun, however, remained the primary means of anti-tank defense. The 88mm gun proved its value in France in 1940 and later against the British in North Africa. Rommel was able to blunt British attacks in the desert by holding important points with units based on anti-tank guns.[82] On the continent the Germans (as well as the Soviets) developed the concept of the Pak (*Panzerabwehrkanone*) front, using anti-tank guns in depth, in a manner very much like that described before the war by writers such as Gallwitz and Nehring.[83] During the war, a Third Panzer Army report listed 75mm and 88mm anti-tank guns as the most effective anti-tank weapons.[84] These tactics proved very effective in thwarting Operation

Goodwood, where a heavy tank assault by Field Marshal Bernard Montgomery's forces foundered on a series of gun lines laid out in depth backed by armored *Kampfgruppen*.[85]

The primacy of the gun in anti-tank defense, aside from its doctrinal basis, was also rooted in the nature of the German Army. The vast majority of the German Army's divisions were "leg" infantry, which had no tanks and relied largely on horses for transport. For these units, the anti-tank gun was their only means of anti-tank defense. Curiously, one of the more interesting aspects of this was the debate during the inter-war period as to whether or not an infantry division's anti-tank guns should be towed by motor vehicles. During the 1920s some writers advocated that if an anti-tank gun was to be effective, it had to move as fast, if not faster, than a tank.[86] Once rearmament began, however, some questioned the wisdom of having anti-tank guns towed by trucks, as that would give them much greater mobility than the rest of the division.[87] Fortunately for the Germans, the anti-tank guns remained motorized.[88] As the war entered its later stages, the Germans also devoted much time to strengthening their anti-tank defense by the use of mines and by hand-fired weapons employed by the infantry. These included the *Panzerfaust*, *Panzerschreck* and *Puppchen*. As these weapons were developed, they were incorporated into and became a regular feature of German anti-tank defenses.[89]

For most of the war, towed anti-tank guns were considered quite adequate as the main means of anti-tank defense.[90] As the war went on, however, Guderian, as Inspector General of Panzer Troops regarded the towed anti-tank gun, especially the 75mm, as being too cumbersome. As early as October 1943 he wanted to replace towed anti-tank guns with either assault guns or later the Panzer Jäger IV.[91] He was able to gain Hitler's agreement on that, but production problems made the fulfillment of such desires impossible.[92]

For Guderian, however, the one thing an assault gun could not replace was a tank. By the autumn of 1943 there was increasing sentiment among front line units to replace tanks with assault guns. Guderian fought this tooth and nail, using arguments that were both truthful and disingenuous. He stressed the fact noted previously that the tank's gun had a 360 degree traverse as opposed to the limited 24 degree traverse of the turretless assault gun. Guderian also argued rather less truthfully, that the assault gun was helpless in close combat because it had no machine gun. Reports from units, especially infantry divisions, which claimed that assault guns were superior to tanks were dismissed by Guderian as being subjective because assault guns normally remained with the infantry, while the tanks were withdrawn for other missions.[93]

Ultimately, the idea of replacing tanks with assault guns was discarded for doctrinal reasons. German doctrine right from the start held that the tank was an offensive weapon.[94] Guderian argued that while in some cases, especially defensive counterattack, the tank could be used like an assault gun, to use the assault gun like a tank in a full-scale offensive operation was simply wrong. The tactical drawbacks of the assault gun eroded the strength of the attacking force. Thus, if the panzer division was to remain the basis of the German Army's offensive power, it in turn had to be based on the tank.[95] In this case, Guderian won his argument.

The ideas propounded in German manuals were not only important in a doctrinal sense, but also in the sense that they were reflective of the attitude of the senior officers under whose auspices they were prepared. The attitude of Beck as Chief of the General Staff toward the development of tanks has already been noted. Equally important was the open-mindedness shown by other senior officers and branches toward the development of tanks. Here again Guderian's memoir is somewhat less than completely honest. Guderian depicted the creation of the panzer arm as a titanic struggle led by him, naturally, against the hidebound older branches, most notably the cavalry, who were dominated by a bunch of crotchety old-timers.[96] To be sure, some senior officers opposed the evolution of the panzer arm. General Max von Poseck, the Chief of Cavalry during the 1920s, fought consistently against tanks, once even arguing that cavalry was better because it could deploy for battle faster than tanks.[97] Officers such as Poseck, however, were rather more the exception than the rule. A more representative approach was shown by Field Marshal Gerd von Rundstedt. At first, after an early exercise, he told Guderian that his ideas on tanks were "nonsense."[98] Once he realized their potential, however, Rundstedt quickly favored their use and became arguably Germany's most successful field commander in World War II.

The cavalry branch also fell in with the prevailing trends pretty quickly. The initial feeling of some officers was that cavalry and tanks could work together. One author argued that this was possible because armored vehicles and cavalry shared the attributes of mobility and the ability to achieve surprise.[99] Subsequent developments showed, however, that this was not possible. Given the reality of the situation, the cavalry, while not abandoning the horse entirely, instituted its own motorization program. By 1939 the cavalry's motorization program resulted in the creation of the light divisions. These units, however, were criticized by Guderian as being flawed organizationally.[100] These defects became apparent in the Polish campaign and were duly noted in the after-action reports of the light divisions after the campaign.[101] As a result, all four light divisions were converted to panzer divisions before the 1940 campaign. It is also worth pointing out that the one cavalry division in the German Army in 1941 was converted to a panzer division after the Barbarossa campaign, although mounted units did not disappear completely.[102] The cavalry also produced some of Germany's best tank commanders, including Fridolin von Senger und Etterlin, Hasso von Manteuffel and Ewald von Kleist, to name a few.

The armor advocates were fortunate not only in having friendly superior officers, but also in having the approval of the supreme authority in Germany after 1933, Adolf Hitler. Tanks and aircraft appealed to him, partly because he was fascinated with what were then considered novel forms of warfare, partly because of his interest in contemporary technology. Guderian noted Hitler's delight at the maneuvers of tank and motorized units.[103] Hitler also showed his support by the appointments of Werner von Blomberg as War Minister and Werner von Fritsch as Commander-in-Chief of the Army. According to Nehring, the creation of the first three panzer divisions in the fall of 1934 was the result of their intervention in February 1934.[104]

Finally, German armor doctrine fit very easily into the broader war-fighting doctrine of the German Army. This is important because it illustrates a subtle yet important difference between German military thought and that of the British theorists. Both Liddell-Hart and Fuller believed that armor operations should be aimed at inducing strategic paralysis in the enemy. Liddell-Hart argued that the Napoleonic method of making the opposing army the objective was wrong. Instead, an army should strike at a moral objective to demoralize the enemy.[105] In keeping with the myth of British influence on the German Army, some authors have argued that these concepts influenced the conduct of German operations.[106]

The idea of inflicting strategic paralysis on the enemy was important to the Germans, but the difference was in emphasis. Whereas Fuller and Liddell-Hart regarded paralysis as an end in itself, for the Germans it was only a means to an end, that being the physical destruction of the enemy's armed forces. This was to be accomplished by the *Vernichtungsschlacht*, the battle of annihilation.

For Clausewitz, the destruction or defeat of the enemy was one of the central objects of any war.[107] Moltke also emphasized this in his writings. This was later refined into the concept of the battle of annihilation, developed by the Chief of the General Staff General Count Alfred von Schlieffen before 1914, based on his study of Hannibal's victory at Cannae.[108] The general climate of opinion in Germany remained convinced of the validity of the concept, with Tannenberg being held up as the model, especially by one of its principal architects.[109] There was the only very occasional challenge to this approach to the conduct of war, but such views did not gain any credence in Germany.[110]

The concept of the battle of annihilation provided the basis for the conduct of German operations during the entire war. The objective was the physical destruction of the enemy army, since it was assumed that decisive battles would ultimately deliver victory. This proved successful in Poland and France, but ultimately broke down in Russia owing to the distances involved and the wide difference in mobility between the motorized units and the regular infantry divisions, which relied on horses for transport.[111] The concepts were still retained, however, well into the late stages of the war. As late as the spring of 1944, for example, Guderian proposed and Hitler accepted the idea of withdrawing a number of panzer and panzer grenadier divisions from various fronts. They were to be assembled into an operational reserve and employed in a large scale offensive on the eastern front.[112] These plans, however, came to naught because of the D-Day landing and the Soviet summer offensive. Nonetheless, the Germans carried on with this right down to the Ardennes offensive of December 1944.

From the preceding pages, it is abundantly clear the German armor doctrine was not strongly influenced at all by the ideas of foreign thinkers, although the Germans were familiar with the ideas of Fuller, de Gaulle and, to a much lesser extent, Liddell-Hart. It is also clear that German armor, anti-tank, and military doctrine in general, was neither new nor innovative, as some have argued.[113] Rather German armor doctrine was simply the perfection and refining of tactics they had developed during the last two years of World War I. German writers openly admitted this. After the French campaign, Colonel Count Schack wrote an article in *Deutsche Wehr* comparing the German offensives of March 1918 and May 1940. He stated quite clearly that what the Germans did in May of 1940 was really no different from what they did in March of 1918. The only difference was the assault divisions had their mobility greatly enhanced by the addition of the internal combustion engine.[114] Likewise, anti-tank doctrine grew out of the German Army's experiences in World War I. These in turn were fitted into the German's Army's broader war-fighting doctrine, which was openly based on the ideas of Clausewitz, Moltke, Schlieffen and Schlichting. Thus, intellectually, the Germany Army of World War II owed much to its imperial predecessor. The unique approach to the problems of armored warfare taken by the Germans allowed them to deploy and use their armored and anti-tank units in a uniquely German manner.

CHAPTER FIVE

German Divisional Organization

"The well-defined cooperation of panzer troops with complementary arms establishes a new, properly trained combined arms unit."
—HEINZ GUDERIAN, 1936[1]

One of the least discussed, but most important, aspects of military affairs is an army's formal organization. How an army's fighting units are organized can often determine the outcome of a campaign. A classic example is Napoleon's use of the *corps d'armee* of several divisions, which gave him a huge advantage over his early Austrian, Prussian and Russian opponents, who still used the unwieldy eighteenth century type of army organization. The same organizational advantage served the German Army's armored force, the strength of which was embodied in the panzer division.

As a military formation, the first panzer division in 1935 was representative of several experiences gained by the German Army both during and after World War I. First, it represented the logical outcome of the German Army's experiments in the 1920s and 1930s to gain mobility by using more motor vehicles. Second, the panzer division represented the persuasive success of a group of officers who advocated, with the tacit assent of Adolf Hitler, the use of tanks en masse. Finally, the division's organization embodied a significant aspect of the German Army's philosophical understanding of war, which called for the use of combined arms to ultimately accomplish what the Germans called the strategy of annihilation (*Vernich-tungstrategie*).

From the start, the panzer division was based on three fundamental principles: the use of tanks in large numbers; their close support by the other arms, such as infantry, artillery and engineers; and finally organizational flexibility about the "mix" of arms. The 1935 division was built around a base element of a two regiment panzer brigade and an infantry regiment, along with supporting units.[2] The panzer regiments each had a two battalion establishment, with each battalion ideally having a combination of light and heavy tanks, with the former predominating.[3] The infantry regiment contained machine gun, motorcycle and engineer elements, as well as heavy weapons. The presence of engineers even extended to the motorcycle and reconnaissance battalions. Further support units included an anti-tank battalion, a light artillery regiment consisting of twelve towed and twelve self-propelled guns, plus a light engineer company and a signal battalion.[4] The division's organization is shown in Figure 5.1 at the end of this chapter.

In the interval between 1935 and 1938, the Germans slightly altered the division's organization, largely by expanding the engineer unit to a full battalion.[5] This organization is shown in Figure 5.2.

At the outbreak of war in 1939, the Germans were able to deploy ninety-eight divisions, but less than half of these were ready for active service. The best trained and equipped elements were few, actually only some five panzer divisions, four motorized infantry divisions and four "light" divisions.[6] The light divisions, being the result of the cavalry's motorization program, were built around a basic structure of two *Kavallerie Schützen* regiments, each consisting of two battalions. The division's tank strength consisted of a single tank battalion composed solely of the very light Pz I and Pz II tanks.[7]

The Polish campaign provided the unblooded German Army with the test of battle that brought a relatively easy victory. The officers who had argued for and created the panzer divisions were pleased with their performance, although Halder noted the frequency of immobilizing traffic jams.[8]

The commanders of the panzer divisions were satisfied with the panzer division as a combat organization. The 1938 manual *Richtlinien für die Führung der Panzer-Division* called for the division to be broken down into combined arms battle groups, or *Kampfgruppen*. Combat experience in Poland confirmed the successful results obtained by this practice. The 2nd Light Division noted in its after-action report on the campaign the efficacy of the battle group organization. The 1st Panzer Division enjoyed similar results with this system of organization. The 3rd Panzer Regiment, while noting the need for improvement in the techniques involved in the implementation of this practice, also noted that the principle itself was quite correct.[9]

One of the newer formations gave the Germans less satisfaction, namely the light division. This unit, which was the result of the cavalry's motorization program, had drawn critical comments from Guderian before the war. In a March 1939 article in *Militärwissenschaftliche Rundschau,* Guderian noted that while the light division had more reconnaissance assets than the panzer division, it had only a fraction of the panzer division's tank strength, thus giving only a limited offensive capability.[10] The German experience in Poland confirmed the validity of Guderian's criticism. The after-action report of the 2nd Light Division (later the 7th Panzer Division) noted that the division was equipped only with the Pz I and Pz II, which the report described as being badly armored and inadequately armed, a view with which Halder agreed completely.[11]

To be sure, there were attempts to save the light division as an organization. The after-action report of the 4th Light Division, while noting the weakness of the present organization suggested that it could be rectified by giving the tank battalion a fourth company, with one platoon of Pz IIIs and three platoons of Pz IVs.[12] Such measures, however, could be no more than a band aid approach to a situation where radical surgery was needed.

Dissatisfied with the light divisions, the Germans reorganized them into panzer divisions. In some cases, this was done by giving each light division an additional tank battalion, thus creating a panzer regiment. In one case, when the 2nd Light Division was reorganized into the 7th Panzer Division, the division received a complete two battalion panzer regiment to go along with its original tank battalion, making a total of three tank battalions for the 1940 campaign.[13]

One of the curious results of the reorganization undertaken between the 1939 and 1940 campaigns was that very few of the panzer divisions now had the same organization. The 1st, 2nd, and 3rd Panzer Divisions had an organization built around a panzer brigade of two regiments, each of which had a different organization. The 4th Panzer Division of two regiments, again with each regiment having a different organization. The 5th Panzer had two panzer regiments and two infantry regiments of the same type, while the 9th Panzer had the same infantry component as the 5th, but only one panzer regiment. The 6th and 8th Panzer Divisions had only one panzer and one infantry regiment, plus a motorcycle battalion. The 10th Panzer had a two regiment panzer brigade and a two regiment infantry brigade.[14]

The Germans also employed as many as four types of infantry regiments. Two had three battalions each, but only one had a heavy weapons company as part of the battalion organization. The other regiments had two battalion organizations, the difference again being the presence or absence of a heavy weapons company. There were also as many as three types of motorcycle battalions, ranging from two to three companies with either a heavy weapons or machine gun company attached or mixed with infantry elements.[15]

The Germans were able to take advantage of the lack of a standard organization by tailoring each division's organization to the operational task assigned to it. This began with the types of tanks employed by each division. Halder discussed the allocation of armor in some detail for the coming French campaign in his diary. He began with the statement that one should not adhere too closely to a rigid order of battle, but that tanks should be given tasks suited to operational necessities. Thus for the drive across Holland, a relatively minor part of the campaign, Pz Is and Pz IIs would do, while panzer divisions assigned to the crucial drive to the Meuse would employ the bulk of the Pz IIIs and Pz IVs.[16]

The notion of a tailored organization extended to the other elements of the divisions. All the divisions that were to be involved in the Meuse crossing, the 1st, 2nd, 5th, 6th, 7th, 8th and 10th Panzer Divisions, had an engineer platoon as part of the divisional reconnaissance battalion. The 1st, 2nd and 10th Panzer Divisions also had a heavy artillery battalion attached in addition to the normal two light artillery battalions. The 9th Panzer Divisions, which had the fewest tanks, but whose drive across Holland was valuable to the Germans as a strategic deception, had two battalions organized into a reconnaissance regiment. The 3rd and 4th Panzer Divisions, part of General Erich Hoepner's XVI Corps, were to play only a minor part in the operation, but make an important contribution by tying up Allied forces in Belgium. For this, however, the divisions could make do largely with Pz Is and Pz IIs.[17] The tank strength of these divisions could vary considerably. The 1st Panzer Division had about 300 tanks, while the 9th possessed a mere 150.[18]

The 1940 campaign in western Europe turned out to be a tremendous success for German arms. The panzer divisions in particular distinguished themselves, commanded by Guderian, and the 7th, commanded by Rommel. The German *Kampfgruppe* method of employing the division's elements showed its value once again.[19] Another important factor was the flexibility shown in the use of weapons, especially the 88mm anti-aircraft gun being used in an anti-tank role. Most importantly, the campaign was not costly. Total German Army casualties for the campaign were 26,972 killed, 113,152 wounded and 13,152 missing.[20] This was a very modest cost compared to the fearful bloodletting of World War I. The panzer divisions in particular were spared heavy losses, even in the most difficult part of the campaign, which lasted from 10-30 May 1940. Guderian's XIX Corps, for example, suffered only 1% killed and 2% wounded. The 1st Panzer Division for the entire campaign lost a total of 45 officers and 448 NCOs and men.[21] This was primarily because of the mobility of the panzer divisions, which allowed them to escape heavy attacks by the slower moving Allies. They were never really able to catch a panzer division with a heavy assault while a panzer division was in a static position. The disorganization and demoralization of the Allied forces also contributed to this.

Even while the Luftwaffe was trying to subdue the Royal Air Force in vain, Hitler was turning his gaze eastward. For the projected invasion of the Soviet Union Hitler, who recognized the offensive power of armor, wanted to increase the number of panzer and motorized infantry divisions. This was eventually officially decreed by OKH on 26 September 1940.[22] The easiest way this could be done was by having the six divisions with two panzer regiments give up a regiment. The four remaining divisions retained their panzer regiment, and new regiments were created for four other divisions.[23]

Most of the new panzer and motorized infantry divisions were reorganized infantry divisions. The 19th, 27th and 33rd Infantry Divisions became the 19th, 17th and 15th Panzer Divisions, respectively, while the 18th and 20th Panzer Divisions were created from unattached units in their respective *Wehrkreise*. The 3rd, 10th, 14th, 18th, 25th and 36th Infantry Divisions were upgraded to motorized infantry divisions. Once the old infantry divisions had received their new equipment, they would turn their now unnecessary material and personnel, such as those involved in the care, handling and feeding of the horses, back to their respective *Wehrkreise* for reassignment.[24]

In addition, all of the existing panzer and motorized infantry divisions at that time were refitted and reorganized. This involved having some units give up one of their two panzer regiments to a new formation. The brigade sub-unit was done away with. The officers and men of the old brigade headquarters provided the command staffs for the new divisions. The 1st Panzer Division, for example, lost the headquarters of its panzer brigade, which was sent to form the division headquarters of the newly forming 18th Panzer Division.[25] In all cases the equipping and manning of the divisions were overseen by the special staffs sent by the OKH Chief of Armaments and the Commander of the Replacement Army.

The time required to complete this reorganization could vary widely from division to division. When the 11th Panzer division was organized, for example, it took from 1 August 1940 to 21 September 1940 to assemble the division's units at its home station of Erfurt in *Wehrkreis* IX. The division was completely equipped and holding large-scale exercises by October 1940.[26] Some other divisions, such as the 10th, 18th and 36th Motorized Infantry Divisions, would not be fully organized and trained until late in the spring of 1941. The biggest delay in completing the reorganization of some divisions was in obtaining equipment. The 10th, 18th and 36th Motorized Infantry Divisions and the 18th and 20th Panzer Divisions, for example, were to receive their vehicles in 25% increments between December 1940 and March 1941.[27]

These changes resulted in most German panzer divisions having a standard organization, as depicted in Figure 5.3. It was based on one panzer regiment of two battalions and two infantry regiments, also of two battalions. The supporting elements were also standardized around an artillery regiment of three battalions, a reconnaissance battalion, plus engineer, signal, anti-tank and anti-aircraft battalions, as well as minor elements, including ordnance, supply and medical units.[28] There were three panzer divisions, however, the 6th, 17th and 20th, that has three tank battalions.[29] There were dissimilarities among these divisions. The 6th Panzer Division's tank element consisted of the 11th Panzer Regiment with two tank battalions, plus an independent tank battalion, the 65th.[30] The 20th Panzer Division, on the other hand, simply had one panzer regiment of three battalions.[31] The end result of this was that the Germans were able to double the number of panzer divisions, even though their total tank part remained virtually static.

The expansion of the number of panzer divisions did, however, generate a good deal of debate, especially after the war. Guderian thought it had a harmful effect, as the effective tank strength of the old two panzer regiment division was halved. This, Guderian felt, was an unwarranted diminution of the division's striking power.[32] General Wilhelm Ritter von Thoma, under whose auspices the reorganization was carried out as he was the Inspector General of Panzer Troops at the time, took the tack of declaring the reorganization harmful, and blamed Hitler for any problems.[33] Guderian's subordinate and fellow armor theorist Walter Nehring disagreed. He thought the reorganization of the panzer divisions was a positive step, as a relatively standard organization for the divisions brought some order to the administrative problems that had arisen from the variety of divisional organizations in 1940.[34]

In fact, each point of view had merit. Nehring was right in the short-term for several reasons. From the point of view of command and control, the new organization made sense. As previously mentioned, in the 1940 campaign some of the divisions possessed over 250 tanks. This, along with such a division's motorized infantry, artillery and support elements, made the division an unwieldy mass of vehicles, often difficult to control. Also any army, in order to be efficiently administered, requires at least a small degree of standardization, especially in matters such as supply and maintenance.

In the long run, however, Guderian also proved to be correct. Even during the 1940 campaign, some divisions reported up to a 50% loss in strength. For a division with about 300 tanks, however, even losses of this magnitude would still leave the division with a formidable offensive capability. Under the new organizational scheme the divisions, especially those with only two tank battalions, rapidly lost their offensive strength if they had to undertake an extended campaign without a long pause for rest and maintenance, as well as a continuous supply of spare parts and replacement vehicles. This became painfully evident during the Russian campaign.

The 1942 summer offensive against the Soviet Union, Operation Barbarossa, provided the German Army with many initial victories. Its ultimate failure, however, left the panzer divisions in a perilous state. Even before the battle of Kiev, serious difficulties were being encountered. Guderian noted that no unit of the XXIV Panzer Corps had been able to devote as much as a single day to rest or maintenance.[35] Losses in the panzer divisions were exacerbated by the fact that the divisions undertook the final offensive against Moscow Operation Typhoon, in a weakened state. By 6 November 1942 the average panzer division could deploy only one-third of its normal strength.[36] By December and January, the combat capability of the panzer arm reached its nadir. Two examples here are most illustrative. By 19 December 1941, the 11th Panzer Division was short 101 tanks and 500 vehicles.[37] During the retreat from Moscow the 6th Panzer Division lost every one of its tanks and anti-tank guns.[38] In fact, during the winter crisis, even the panzer divisions had to rely on horse-drawn sled columns, the only sure means of transport in the harsh winter conditions.[39]

For the 1942 summer campaign the Germans required a large armored force to implement Operation Blue. German industry, however, could not make good the losses in equipment suffered during the previous year. To compensate for this and to reinforce the mobile divisions slated for Operation Blue, OKH decided that those divisions remaining in Army Groups North and Center would give up one of their panzer battalions.[40] These would either go to the panzer divisions in Army Groups A and B or to their motorized infantry divisions to give them some added punch. The 1st Panzer Division in April 1942, for example, gave up the 1st Battalion of its panzer regiment to the 16th Motorized Infantry Division.[41]

This drastic measure meant that the Germans once more had divisions with several different organizations. In southern Russia, panzer divisions had three tank battalions, and the motorized infantry divisions had one. On the rest of the Russian front, panzer divisions had only one tank battalion, while the panzer divisions in the west had two. In North Africa, Rommel generally switched elements of the 15th and 21st Panzer Divisions back and forth between the divisions as the situation demanded.

The course of the Stalingrad campaign is too well-known to bear repeating here. After the Stalingrad disaster, OKH began rebuilding the three panzer divisions (the 14th, 16th and 24th) as well as the three motorized infantry divisions (3rd, 29th and 60th) lost there and replacing the battalions given up by the divisions in Army Group Center and North. This was normally done when a panzer division was pulled out of the line for refitting. The 1st Panzer Division, for example, as part of its rebuilding in France in early 1943, reconstituted its missing panzer battalion that had been given up in April 1942 to the 16th Motorized Infantry Division.[42]

For the Kursk offensive that began on 5 July 1943, the Germans again reinforced some of their panzer divisions with a third tank battalion, consisting now of the formidable Tiger tank. The other two battalions used a variety of tanks. Most panzer divisions had battalions equipped with the Pz III or Pz IV.[43] One or two divisions, such as the 11th Panzer Division, in addition to a battalion of Tigers, also had a battalion of Pz IVs and a battalion of new Panther tanks.[44] The three battalion scheme was only a temporary measure. The Tiger tank was a rare commodity to begin with, and the Germans suffered heavy tank losses in the battle. After Kursk, Tiger battalions were employed only as corps or army assets. Furthermore, the three battalion organization apparently applied only to the divisions in Army Group South. The 2nd Panzer Division, part of Army Group Center, for example, had only two tank battalions, one of Pz IIIs and one of Pz IVs.[45] The Tiger tanks that operated on that part of the front were those designed by Porsche. They were organized into two battalions and attached to Colonel General Walter Model's Ninth Army, where they proved to be a total failure.[46]

Marked similarities can be observed between the development of the Army panzer divisions and that of the SS panzer divisions. Before the war the only large SS unit was the SS *Verfügungstruppe* (special duty unit), which was fully motorized.[47] There was also the *Leibstandarte Adolf Hitler*, a regimental size bodyguard for the protection of the Führer under his old Nazi Party crony, SS Colonel Josef "Sepp" Dietrich, as well as units of concentration camp personnel, namely the SS *Totenkopfverbande*, under the sinister SS General Theodor Eicke, head of the concentration camp system and one-time commandant of Dachau.

For the Polish campaign, the *Leibstandarte Adolf Hitler* was employed as a regimental combat team broken down into battle groups.[48] The SS *Verfügungstruppe* was combined with the 7th Panzer Regiment and some other Army units to form an ad hoc unit called Panzer Division Kempf, which was something between a reinforced panzer brigade and a weak panzer division.[49] The Germans were able to mix such units because of the uniform training conducted by both SS and Army units, based on Army manuals.[50]

In 1940 the SS *Verfügungstruppe*, having been expanded to a full division, was committed to the offensive against France. Eicke was able to organize the SS *Totenkopf* Division from current or former concentration camp personnel. This unit was also committed to the French campaign, as was Dietrich's SS *Leibstandarte Adolf Hitler*, now expanded by attached units to a brigade-size motorized infantry unit.[51]

After the French campaign the Waffen SS (Armed SS) was further expanded. The SS *Leibstandarte Adolf Hitler* was raised to a full division. The SS *Verfügungstruppe* was broken up and its component regiments used in the formation of two other divisions, the SS *Das Reich* and the SS *Wiking*. Another SS division, the SS *Polizei*, was formed from the uniformed German police, along with the SS *Nord*. All of these divisions saw action in the Russian campaign of 1941.[52] With the exceptions of the SS *Polizei* and the SS *Nord*, all of the SS divisions were fully motorized and patterned on the organization of an Army motorized infantry division. They were based on three regiments of three battalions each, plus divisional engineer, reconnaissance, artillery, and anti-tank and signal units.[53] This organization is shown in Figure 5.4.

Following Barbarossa's failure in December 1941, the SS *Leibstandarte Adolf Hitler* and SS *Das Reich Division*s were withdrawn from the front and sent to France. A new SS *Totenkopf* Division was being formed, and its personnel would be augmented by the original division's survivors who were extricated from the Demyansk pocket.[54] The SS *Wiking* Division was part of the First Panzer Army's drive to the Caucasus, while the SS *Polizei* Division remained in Army Group North, and the SS *Nord* Division was reorganized into the 8th SS Cavalry Division (*Florian Geyer*). Most SS division's received newly formed tank battalions as a matter of course in the spring of 1942.[55] During the autumn of 1942 these divisions were designated as panzer grenadier divisions.[56] The armor element of these units was expanded to a full tank regiment of two battalions by the time of Kursk. Between the autumn of 1943 and the summer of 1944 these units were redesignated as panzer divisions.[57]

By June 1944 the Army could field some twenty-three panzer divisions and the SS an additional seven. The strength of these units, however, fluctuated widely. Since the SS infantry regiments had one more battalion than their Army counterparts, the SS panzer divisions had considerably more infantry. In Normandy in June 1944, for example, the 2nd Panzer Division had an authorized strength of 16,313 officers, NCOs and men.[58] In contrast, the 1st SS Panzer Division (*Adolf Hitler*) mustered over 21,000 officers, NCOs and men.[59]

Tank strength also varied widely. The *Panzer Lehr* Division, an elite Army formation consisting of units drawn from training schools, possessed some 229 tanks and assault guns by 1 June 1944, a slight surplus over its authorized strength of 227.[60] The 1st SS Panzer Division (*Adolf Hitler*), although its table of organization and equipment called for it to have some 203 tanks, had only 80 Pz IVs and Panthers ready for action by 1 June 1944. The shortfall was partially made up by the division's having a full complement of assault guns.[61] The 1st SS Panzer's sister division, the 12th SS Panzer Division (*Hitler Jugend*), had 140 of its authorized 186 tanks ready.[62] The difference between the Army and SS panzer divisions is clearly shown in Figures 5.5 and 5.6.

As a consequence of the military disasters suffered in both the east and west in the summer of 1944, the Germans made three changes in the organization of their armor units. First, in July 1944 the Germans created ad hoc panzer brigades. The organization of these brigades could vary widely. A simple brigade was composed, at least in theory, of a tank battalion with either 36 Pz IVs or Panthers, and an infantry battalion and engineer company. A brigade was also supposed to have a maintenance workshop.[63] The 10th Panzer Brigade, formed in the late summer of 1944, was composed of six tank battalions and one tank destroyer battalion drawn from both Army and SS units.[64] Later three other brigades were formed with two battalions of tanks and infantry each, plus anti-tank, engineer and reconnaissance elements.[65]

The experiment was tried in the west in the late summer and autumn of 1944. The brigades were to act as a flexible mobile reserve for use over a wide front. They were to be able to rapidly attack and destroy any enemy units that had broken through the front.[66] The scheme proved to be a complete failure. Most of the brigades were tank-heavy, poorly trained, and often thrown into situations where they could do little in the face of overwhelming Allied superiority. Many of the brigades lacked an organic maintenance unit. Thus, when a brigade's tanks broke down or were damaged, they had to depend on the charity of another unit for salvage and repair. Units that did have maintenance personnel received them at the expense of the refitting panzer divisions. To spread maintenance personnel around to so many units was a terrible waste of rare and valuable personnel assets. Lieutenant General Edgar Feuchtinger, the commander of the 21st Panzer Division in the Normandy campaign, considered the brigades to be a complete waste of men and material.[67] The brigades were disbanded and incorporated into the existing divisions by the winter of 1944.

The second change was the creation of the unitary panzer corps. This was really a permanent marriage of two weak panzer divisions to form a strong unit with a reduced logistical tail. In many ways, this development was precisely the kind of consolidation that Guderian had warned against in late 1943, which he saw as weakening the panzer arm.[68] Four of these corps were formed: *Gross Deutschland, Feldherrnhalle*, XXIV and XL. This also proved a failure, as the "creation" of merely four panzer formations by that late date was in no way going to affect the outcome of the war.[69]

The last change was a reorganization of the panzer division. Initially proposed in March 1945, the purpose of the reorganization was to address the crushing shortages of vehicles and fuel. The panzer regiment had one of its tank battalions replaced with a battalion of mechanized infantry with 520 men, mounted in a combination of 47 half-tracks and 35 trucks. The tank battalion had four companies, two of Pz IVs and two of Panthers. The two battalion panzer grenadier regiment was rather inaptly named, as the regiment, which included artillery and engineer elements, had a total of 3,694 men and only 290 trucks. The division's transport was augmented by horses, to be serviced by a veterinary platoon. Altogether, the 1945 division would have almost as many trucks as the 1944 division, but only 54 tanks, and considerably fewer reconnaissance vehicles and 11,402 men as compared with the 13,213 men authorized in the 1944 division's organization.[70]

It should be noted, however, that this organization applied only to Army units, at least officially. The SS divisions went through a somewhat different reorganization. They retained the two battalion tank regiment, but the infantry regiments were reduced to two battalions each.[71] Although the division was supposed to be fully motorized, the shortage of vehicles, fuel, and drivers was so widespread that it was very likely that SS divisions were forced to use horses for transport as well.

If any conclusion is possible from the preceding pages, it would certainly be that the Germans never really employed a standard divisional organization. It is interesting to note that the 1938 manual for the employment of the panzer division, *Richtlinien für die Führung der Panzer Division,* had an organizational diagram at the end of the manual.[72] This is missing from the 1940 edition, *Richtlinien für Führung und Einsatz der Panzer Division,* even though by that time the German were actually employing, at least officially, a standard organization.[73]

The same could be said for the way in which the Germans operated their divisions in the field. The 1938 manual stressed the importance of the principle of combined arms. It was recommended that when moving, the division should be broken down into march groups of all arms.[74] In the field this translated into the *Kampfgruppe,* or battle group. They could vary considerably in size. For a full strength division, such units could be based on regiments. On 25 June 1941, for example, the 11th Panzer Division on the eastern front was divided into two *Kampfgruppen. Kampfgruppe* Angern was based on the 110th and 111th Infantry Regiments, supported by the division's artillery, anti-tank and anti-aircraft units. *Kampfgruppe* Riebel was composed of the 15th Panzer Regiment and the division's reconnaissance battalion. Both Kampfgruppen had engineers.[75]

The make-up of these two *Kampfgruppen* is worth examining in some detail, as it reflects the expression of German doctrine in organizing combat units. Both Kampfgruppen had an anti-tank capability, as well as infantry. While *Kampfgruppe* Angern had the divisional artillery for support, *Kampfgruppe* Riebel could make do with the tanks using their main guns in an artillery role. The Pz III, for example, normally carried fifty-nine high explosive shells, thirty-six anti-tank shells and five other shells of various types. Later models of the Panzer III, while somewhat more heavily armored and slightly upgunned, was still able to carry a comparable ammunition load.[76] Finally, the engineers could be used to neutralize mine fields or fortifications.

Kampfgruppen could also be based on battalions, and in dire straits even companies. A good example of this was the 10th Panzer Division. By the onset of the winter of 1941, the balance of the 10th Panzer Division's strength was located in *Kampfgruppe* Baumgart, consisting of a motorcycle company, a tank company, an infantry company and two troops of 88nim guns.[77]

The Germans continued this practice throughout the war and on all fronts. In the east some representative examples would be the 1st Panzer Division's counterattack of 6 December 1943 and the 6th Panzer Division's attack to aid the escape of the Vilna garrison in July 1944.[78] In the west, the exploits of the 21st Panzer Division's *Kampfgruppe* von Luck that stymied Operation Goodwood are well-known.[79] After suffering heavy losses in the first two months of the Normandy campaign, the Panzer Lehr division was divided into three combined arms Kampfgruppen to support several of the Seventh Army's corps over a wide front.[80] Perhaps the most famous, or infamous, unit was *Kampfgruppe* Peiper. This force, which was composed of about 4,000 men from the 1st SS Panzer Division (*Adolf Hitler*), was to lead Sepp Dietrich's 6th Panzer Army's thrust to the Meuse River. It included 102 tanks, evenly divided between Pz IVs, Panthers and Tigers, five flak tanks, a self-propelled flak battalion equipped with 20mm guns, twenty-five self-propelled guns, a truck-towed 105mm artillery battalion and a battalion of SS mechanized infantry. It also had reconnaissance elements and two companies of engineers.[81]

The Germans even extended this principle to forming ad hoc units from several formations. Three excellent examples of this are Panzer Division Kempf, Panzer Brigade Eberbach and *Korpsgruppe* Fischer Panzer Division Kempf presents an interesting case, as it was a combination of Army and SS units. In August of 1939 the Germans formed Panzer Division Kempf, as mentioned previously, around the 7th Panzer Regiment and the SS *Deutschland* Regiment, with other units provided either by the Army or the SS *Verfügungstruppe*. It fought in Poland before being officially disbanded on 7 October 1939.[82]

Panzer Brigade Eberbach was formed in November 1941 by Guderian to save as much gasoline as possible for the advance on Tula. Guderian pooled all the tanks from the 3rd and 4th Panzer Divisions, paired them up with the *Gross Deutschland* Infantry Regiment, and placed it under the command of Colonel Hans Eberbach, commander of the 4th Panzer Division's panzer regiment.[83] The unit then operated as such for the better part of a month. For immediate support the brigade relied on the heavy weapons of the *Gross Deutschland* Infantry Regiment. It was disbanded in December and the units returned to their parent formations.

Korpsgruppe Fischer was formed as part of the German attempt to prevent the Allies from completing a rapid occupation of Tunisia. In this case the 10th Panzer Division was teamed up with the 334th Infantry Division and one regiment of the Luftwaffe's Hermann Göring Panzer Division. The *Korpsgruppe* was then broken down into four *Kampfgruppen* of varying sizes. The tanks were evenly divided among two of them, *Kampfgruppe* Weber and *Kampfgruppe* Lang. All four *Kampfgruppen* had infantry, artillery, anti-tank, anti-aircraft and engineer elements. It is interesting to note that of the two *Kampfgruppen* with tanks, *Kampfgruppe* Weber had some forty-three Pz III tanks armed with the long 50mm guns, while *Kampfgruppe* Lang, having only thirty-two such Pz IIIs, had eight Tigers as opposed to *Kampfgruppe* Weber's four Tigers.[84] The Germans were able to put together units made up of such diverse elements because of the fact that in all matters of training and doctrine concerning tanks, policy for all branches was set by the office of the Inspector General of Panzer Troops.[85]

The Germans practice of utilizing their divisions in this manner had several effects, some intentional and some accidental. First, the *Kampfgruppe* concept allowed the Germans maximum latitude for "tailoring" forces for specific missions. Also, the combined arms nature of the *Kampfgruppe* allowed it to undertake almost any type of mission. The only other army to come very close to this was the U.S. Army with its concept of the "Combat Command."[86] The practice, however, did not come up to the expectations of theory, primarily because in the field, the U.S. Combat Command was based on a permanent "marriage" of a tank battalion and an infantry battalion.[87] Since these units became the permanent basis of the combat command, the combat command's combat capability would decrease considerably if the base elements suffered heavy casualties. The American organization was also hurt by the inability to develop a uniform armor doctrine for the entire army.[88] In addition the Commander of the Army Ground Forces, General Leslie J. McNair, was a very severe critic of armored divisions and fought against their employment.[89] Throughout the war, the German system remained more flexible, in that their ability to mix and match units in forming *Kampfgruppen* was much greater than the U.S. Army's. The British did experiment in North Africa with the small, mobile "Jock Columns," but this was strictly an improvization and apparently used only in North Africa.[90] After suffering heavy losses in the early part of the war, the Soviets were also able to develop armored and mechanized formations employing combined arms concepts. Such units, while reasonably effective in the Soviet context, never quite came up to German standards. They were also hurt by the tremendous manpower losses suffered by the Russians earlier in the war.[91]

Another advantage derived by the Germans from their system was that it allowed them to minimize the number of headquarters personnel in a division. By organizing the division into several self-contained combined arms units using all of the division's subordinate units, the Germans were able to maintain a division headquarters with a relatively small staff.[92]

Finally, the Germans enjoyed one probably unintended advantage as a result of their system. The *Kampfgruppe* system allowed the Germans to obtain maximum use of their divisions, even after they had taken heavy losses and received few replacements. The 10th Panzer Division, for example, having seen extensive service in the 1941 Russian campaign and having suffered heavy casualties, was reorganized on 20 December 1941. Its main strength was now concentrated in *Kampfgruppe von der Chevallerie*. It contained infantry, tanks, artillery, engineers and other elements, and was manned by men combed out of the division's rear services.[93] This type of organization was to prove very effective in Normandy in 1944, as the Germans had to fight against heavy odds. The bocage country, with its thick hedgerows, also helped the Germans in this battle, as it confined Allied armored thrusts largely to the roads, which the Germans could hold with small combined arms *Kampfgruppen*.[94]

The Germans even used this system for shattered units rebuilding in France. By 31 March 1943 when the 14th Panzer Division was rebuilt after Stalingrad, the division had only about 6,000 men.[95] These, however, were concentrated into a Kampfgruppe and equipped with captured French tanks.[96] This gave it more than enough strength to undertake internal security missions in occupied territory.

In terms of higher units, the Germans tended to group their panzer and motorized infantry units together, something that had been planned as early as 1935.[97] Since these units, including the SS, never amounted to more than 25% of the total number of divisions in the Wehrmacht, to distribute them among the infantry divisions that used horse-drawn transport would have been the height of foolishness. Thus the Germans grouped their mobile divisions into units successively termed first army corps, then motorized corps and finally panzer corps.[98]

The Germans also tended to utilize a unit composed of two or more panzer corps called a panzer group. This was first done in the 1940 campaign when General Hans-Georg Reinhardt's XXXIX Corps and Guderian's XIX Corps were paired up and placed under the command of a panzer group staff commanded by Colonel General Ewald von Kleist.[99] For the later stages of the campaign a second panzer group was formed and placed under Guderian's command.[100]

For the invasion of the Soviet Union, the Germans employed four such panzer groups. Sometimes equipment considerations played an important part in determining the divisions that would compose the group's subordinate corps. All of the component divisions of the Third Panzer Group, for example, had either Czech tanks or French vehicles.[101] In this way the Germans hoped to minimize the spare parts problem with regard to the large number of foreign vehicles they used.

In the field, the panzer groups generally operated as independent entities, subordinate only to army group command. On only one occasion, the Smolensk encirclement of July 1941, were Guderian's Second and Colonel General Hermann Hoth's Third Panzer Groups subordinated to Field Marshal Gunther von Kluge's Fourth Army, something that made the panzer generals extremely unhappy for doctrinal and personal reasons.[102]

In the autumn and winter of 1941–1942, the panzer groups were reorganized. On 6 October 1941 the First and Second Panzer Groups were redesignated as Panzer Armies.[103] The Third and Fourth Panzer Groups were also redesignated as armies on 2 January 1942.[104] This was unquestionably a mistake, as these units now incorporated a higher number of marching infantry divisions that depended on horse-drawn transport. This arrangement had already been tried in the Yugoslavia campaign, when several infantry divisions had been subordinated to the First Panzer Group, with what the Germans considered less than satisfactory results. The quartermaster of the First Panzer Group recommended against the repeating of such an experiment.[105] Liddell-Hart thought that this contributed in no small part to the escape of the Soviet forces in the Don Bend from German encirclement in the summer of 1942, an opinion shared by Hoth.[106]

It is interesting to note that once the term "panzer" was applied to a higher unit, it remained with that unit, regardless of whether or not it had panzer or panzer grenadier divisions. In the Kursk offensive in July 1943, for example, the XLVI

Panzer Corps, part of the Ninth Army, did not possess a single panzer or panzer grenadier division.[107]

The organization of the panzer division is important in itself as it gave the Germans an important advantage over their opponents. This was due primarily to the fact that the German panzer division contained large infantry and engineer elements. If one looks at the organization of the French Division *Cuirassee Reserve* (DCR), for example, the lack of infantry is striking, although the French did better with the more balanced Division *Legere Mechanique* (DLM).[108] The various British armored division organizations, especially early in the war, were also marked by a lack of infantry. The 1940 British armored division, for example, had over 260 tanks but only 1,580 infantry.[109] Although the British reorganized their armored divisions several times during the war, their organization was consistently hurt by a lack of infantry.[110] As for the Russians, the heavy losses suffered in the early stages of the 1941 campaign forced them to organize their tanks into tank-heavy brigades that were dispersed among the infantry divisions. Later on the tank corps and the mechanized corps were reintroduced, both of which proved to be effective organizations.[111] The American organization has already been commented on.

None of these units proved to be quite as effective as those organized by the Germans. Thus much like Napoleon, the German Army owed much of its initial military success to a superior organization of their most important offensive units, the panzer and motorized infantry divisions.

LEGEND FOR FIGURES

Unit Size

XX	Division
X	Brigade
III	Regiment
II	Battalion
I	Company
•••	Platoon

Unit Type

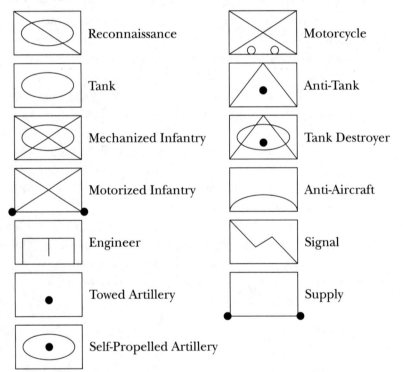

These symbols are considered standard by NATO. They should contribute to the easy understanding of the following figures.

Figure 5.1
The 1935 Panzer Division

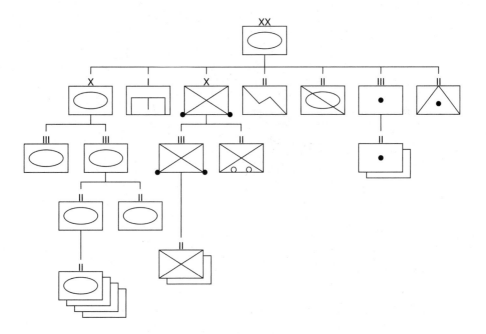

The division's organization is somewhat more complex than
the figure shows.[112] The tank battalions had one company of
heavy tanks each, while the other three companies had light
tanks. Also the infantry battalions had motorcycle, engineer,
machine gun and anti-tank elements. Nevertheless, the figure
gives a clear indication of the direction the Germans were
headed in at the time. An exercise conducted with this type
of division in August 1935 involved about 13,000 officers and
men, including around 7,000 infantry. Its mobility was provided by 4,025 wheeled vehicles and 481 tracked vehicles, the
majority of which were tanks.[113] The division's major supporting element was its light artillery regiment, with twenty-four
105mm towed guns.[114]

Figure 5.2
The 1938 Panzer Division

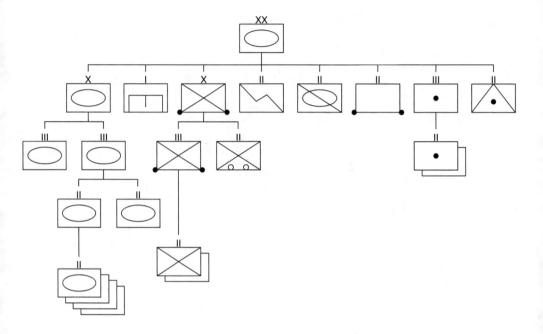

The 1938 division has marked similarities to the 1935 division, but there are important differences.[115] The tank battalions have only three companies, which have a mix of light and medium tanks. Between 1938 and the beginning of the war, an extra infantry regiment was added to the infantry brigade. Also the engineer element was expanded. The type of establishment was used by the original panzer divisions until the reorganization of late 1940.

Figure 5.3
The 1941 Panzer Division

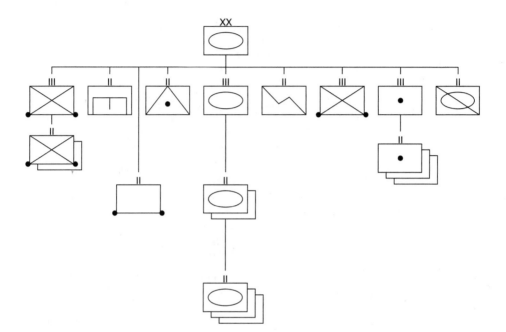

This was the organization used by the Germans for the 1941 campaign, again with several exceptions.[116] As usual, the organization is slightly more complex than the figure indicates. Each tank battalion had one company of medium tanks, mainly Pz IIIs or Pz IVs, and two companies of Pz IIs. Altogether, the division should have had anywhere from 120 to 140 tanks. The infantry regiments contained motorcycle and engineer elements. Also of interest is the proportion of the various arms to each other. The proportionate increase of infantry to tanks helped give it more staying power. The division's artillery support had been increased to a three-battalion artillery regiment. Ideally, the division should have at full strength twenty-four 105mm guns, plus twelve 150mm guns, all truck-towed.[117] It is easy to see how the *Kampfgruppe* concept could be applied to this unit.

Figure 5.4
The 1941 SS Motorized Division

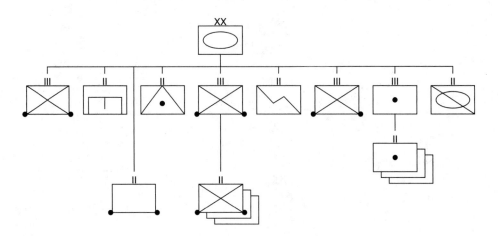

This unit was patterned on the Army motorized infantry division, but with two important differences.[118] First, the SS used a three-battalion regiment down to 1945. Later, one of the infantry regiments was converted to a panzer regiment with two battalions.

Figure 5.5
The 1944 Panzer Division

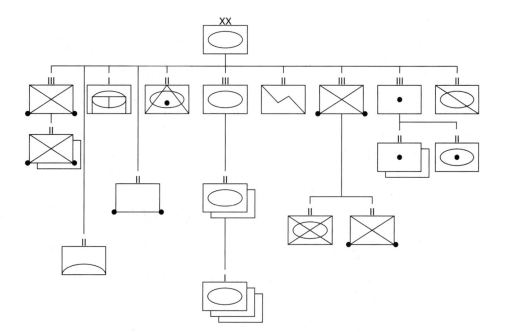

Ideally, the division should have had between 13,500 and 14,000 officers and men and about 160 tanks, but that was rare.[119] The panzer regiment was supposed to have one battalion of Pz IVs and one of Panthers, although again even the number of authorized tanks could vary from division to division.[120] The tank destroyer battalion had a combination of towed anti-tank guns, usually 75mm, and assault guns or tank destroyers. While the number of artillery pieces remained about the same, firepower was increased by the addition of a large number of 80mm and 120mm mortars. Although much more of the division was armored than previous versions, the vast majority of the units still had to rely on soft-skinned vehicles for transport. The infantry regiments still had their own engineer companies.

Figure 5.6
The 1944 SS Panzer Division

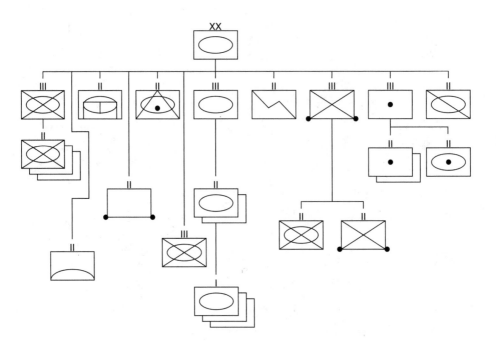

The difference here from its Army counterpart is quite clear.[121] Aside from having two more battalions of infantry (almost 1,000 men), the infantry enjoyed a much greater degree of mechanization. Also the tank destroyer battalion consisted of both assault guns and tank destroyers. Additionally, the panzer regiment had its own anti-aircraft elements. One can easily see why these powerful units were the "fire brigades" of the Germany Army.

CHAPTER SIX

Conclusion

> "The panzer division can be employed together with other motorized and nonmotorized units over large areas as well as independently accomplishing operational missions."
>
> —GERMAN ARMY, 1938[1]

Can any overall conclusions be drawn from the preceding pages as to the German panzer arm, divisional organization, and the German Army in general? In terms of a broad conclusion one can reach, it is that in many ways, the German Army of World War II was more attuned to the nineteenth century than to the twentieth. The inability of the German economy to produce the necessary numbers of vehicles and more importantly, the gasoline needed to run them, forced the German Army to remain heavily dependent on horses for the bulk of its transport.[2]

The German Army approach to war and its broad war-fighting doctrine were also rooted in the nineteenth century. The great focus was on the battle of annihilation. The German Army, taking its cue from Clausewitz, from the elder Moltke on heartily endorsed the very strategy rejected so strongly by the panzer arm's alleged British guru Liddell-Hart in *The Remaking of Modern Armies*.[3]

The German economy's inability to meet the vehicular needs of the Army had a profound effect on the panzer arm. To begin with, it almost certainly created the need for panzer divisions at all, since it would have been wasteful in the extreme to spread the tanks about the large number of infantry divisions that relied on horse-drawn transport. Had the Germans been able to create a completely motorized force, the German Army in this sense would probably have borne a strong resemblance to the U.S. Army. Certainly this was what Beck had in mind. He wanted a smaller, but completely motorized force.[4] Failure to obtain this due to the rapidity of the Army's expansion forced him to do the next best thing, which was to create the panzer arm. This is turn had the effect of essentially dividing the German Army into two distinct parts, a small, motorized force and a large, non-motorized force.[5] While this did not produce insurmountable difficulties in the 1939–1940 campaigns, the invasion of the Soviet Union (with its vast land spaces and poor transportation net) quickly demonstrated the limitations of such a force.[6]

Although somewhat speculative, the question must be asked: could the Germans have produced the vehicles and fuel in sufficient quantities to completely motorize the Army? The answer to this question must undoubtedly be no. Germany simply did not have the resources to create an air force, a navy and a fully motorized army. Hitler might have been able to motorize a larger part of the Army if he decided not to build a navy, and instead devote more resources to the production of tanks and motor vehicles. This point had been made at least in an article in *Militär Wochenblatt* in 1935.[7] Given Hitler's designs against the western powers, especially Britain, however, there was no way he could avoid building a navy as part of his armament programs.[8] In addition, even if the requisite numbers of vehicles could be produced, Germany could not obtain the oil needed to fuel them. The following statistics tell a great deal about the German fuel situation: in December 1940, at the height of her military success, Germany, her Axis allies and the occupied territories possessed 4.1% of the world's oil refining capacity, compared to 21.5% for the Allies and 73% for the neutrals, which included at the time the United States and the Soviet Union.[9] All these things created serious problems in maintaining tank and vehicle strength in the panzer divisions, particularly in the latter stages of the war.

The personnel policies used to man the Army's panzer and motorized divisions were the same as those employed by the rest of the German Army. These policies did have some effect on the panzer arm, as they provided the criteria by which it could be decided whether a destroyed division would be rebuilt or not. The examples of the 10th Panzer Division and the divisions destroyed at Stalingrad have already been discussed. The major factor in the area of personnel was the lack of people with exposure to, or knowledge of, automotive devices. This undoubtedly put the Germans at a disadvantage when it came to producing drivers. In addition, the German Army mistakenly assumed that maintenance units could be staffed by simply drafting civilian auto mechanics directly into units without some prior training in tank repair.[10]

Training also affected the panzer arm. German Army training, and that of the SS as well, stressed the importance of combined arms, no matter what type of unit an individual served in. This was especially important in the German Army, since it was composed of such disparate elements. The ability to keep all the branches of the Army "on the same sheet of music" in terms of training was vital to the successful employment of such ad hoc units as the Panzer Brigade Eberbach and *Korpsgruppe* Fischer.

It is important to note, however, that the training of panzer and mobile units was effected by several factors as the war went on. Training, for instance, was severely hindered later in the war by shortages of both vehicles and fuel. This, along with the need for replacements, forced the Germans to reduce training time for their recruits. The soldiers who were "shortchanged" in training quickly became casualties, creating the need for more replacements and thus establishing a vicious circle. Finally, the invasion of France in 1944 deprived the Germans of a quiet area where they could reform, rest and refit shattered divisions. The demands of both fronts and the lack of quiet made the rehabilitation of divisions very difficult. It was only with the greatest difficulty that OKW was able to amass some eight panzer and two panzer grenadier divisions for the opening of the Ardennes offensive in December 1944, but even this imposing array was backed up by only 970 tanks and assault guns.[11]

For the panzer arm, as well as for the rest of the German Army, doctrine was the cornerstone. German armor doctrine, as stated previously, was the outgrowth of the German Army's experiences in the later stages of World War I. It also fit into the broader German warfighting doctrine, which was based on the Napoleonic concept of achieving the destruction of the enemy's army through the decisive battle.

The panzer division was conceived within these two concepts as a combined arms force which enhanced the Army's ability to conduct operations in accordance with its doctrine. Since equipment deficiencies mandated the division of the German Army into two distinct parts, one motorized and the other not, the panzer arm represented the only means by which the Germans could achieve the kind of strategic penetration that had eluded them in 1918. In the German Army's most successful campaigns, the panzer and motorized infantry divisions represented the Army's cutting edge and created the conditions by which the opposing army could be destroyed.

Doctrine was absolutely vital to the German Army, because all other things flowed from it. The effect of doctrine on training was undeniable. The ability of the German Army to have the most dissimilar elements trained with doctrinal consistency reflected two things. First, it reflected the fact that the German Army's broad, basic doctrine was very close to its armor doctrine. Both emphasized the same principles. Second, it reflected the power of the office of the Inspector General of Panzer Troops, especially when Guderian made the principles of armor doctrine training binding on all units in the Replacement Army.[12] This was vital in allowing horse-drawn marching infantry divisions to work well with panzer divisions in various situations. This was a great advantage because it was something that eluded Germany's opponents.

The U.S. Army lacked a consistent armor doctrine to begin with, and most infantry divisions had precious little training with tanks.[13] British attempts to have infantry and armored divisions work together in tandem in North Africa produced nothing but a series of disastrous failures. This was generally due to a lack of training, but there was also a great deal of confusion over the tank's role in combat.[14] The Russians also suffered from the same kind of problems early on, but they were able eventually to develop their own version of combined arms doctrine.

All of these influences contributed to the manner in which the Germans organized, deployed and operated their panzer divisions. Several conclusions can be drawn from the available evidence. The first is that the Germans never employed any kind of standardized divisional organization. This was true even during the period before the 1941 Russian campaign, when the Germans undertook a reform precisely to standardize their divisional organization. In the field, it is fairly clear that the division was used only as an administrative organization. The basic elements of the division were broken down into combined arms Kampfgruppen. These were consistently mixed and matched to fit the existing situation.

The German ability to do this constituted a great advantage over their opponents. The failures of the tank-heavy British armored divisions and the French DCR have already been noted. The various versions of the U.S. Army's armored division also suffered from a shortage of infantry.[15] Since the panzer and motorized infantry divisions provided the German Army's cutting edge, it can certainly be argued that Germany's flexible divisional organization, and its superiority over the divisional organizations employed by their enemies, was a key element in the Army's victorious campaigns, as well as in its ability to stave off or delay defeat.

One can also draw a general conclusion about the German Army from this study. The German Army often presents the image of a highly mechanized force, the epitome of mechanized warfare in the mid-twentieth century. The evidence, however, clearly demonstrates that this was not the case. Given the fact that the German Army of the twentieth century derived so much from the nineteenth century, one can say that the panzer arm was the most modern element of what was in many ways a pre-modern army.

Notes

INTRODUCTION

1. B. H. Liddell-Hart, *The German Generals Talk* (New York, 1948), p. 90.
2. For purposes of simplicity and consistency, the word panzer will be used interchangeably with both tank and armor.
3. General Heinz Guderian, *Panzer Leader* (New York, 1952), p. 20.
4. The matter of the German Army's reliance on horses is discussed in R. L. DiNardo, *Mechanized Juggernaut or Military Anachronism?: Horses and the German Army of World War II* (Westport, 1991).

CHAPTER ONE

1. Guderian, *Panzer Leader*, p. 29. The statement quoted was supposedly made by Hitler when he saw tanks on maneuvers for the first time.
2. Quoted in Gordon Craig, *Germany, 1866–1945* (New York, 1978), p. 613.
3. Memo From Guderian to Hitler to be Presented at Führer Conference on 20 October 1943, 19 October 1943, National Archives Records Administration Microfilm Series T-78, roll 720, Frame 000392. (Hereafter cited as NARA T-78/720/000392).
4. Quoted in Albert Seaton, *Stalin as Military Commander* (New York, 1976), p. 265.
5. Liddell-Hart, *History of the Second World War* (New York, 1972), p. 23. One might add uranium and tungsten to this list as well.

6. Berenice A. Carroll, *Design For Total War* (The Hague, 1968), p. 145.

7. R. J. Overy, *War and Economy in the Third Reich* (London, 1994), p. 98.

8. Hans-Erich Volkmann, "Die NS Wirtschaft unter dem 'Neuen Plan,'" Militärgeschichtlichen Forschungsamt, *Das Deutsche Reich und der Zweite Weltkrie* (Stuttgart, 1979–1990), Vol. 1, p. 261.

9. Rolf Wagenführ, *Die Deutsche Industrie im Kriege, 1939–1945* (Berlin, 1955), p. 54.

10. State Office of Economic Planning, The Importance of Economic Raw Materials of Southeastern Europe For the German Economy, March 1939, NARA T-84/80/1367770.

11. Volkmann, "Die NS Wirtschaft unter dem "Neuen Plan,'" Militärgeschichtlichen Forschungsamt, *Das Deutsche Reich und der Zweite Weltkrieg,* Vol. 1, p. 271.

12. Brian R. Mitchell, *European Historical Statistics, 1750–1975* (2nd Edition) (New York, 1981), pp. 393–394.

13. Robert Goralski and Russell W. Freeburg, *Oil and War* (New York, 1987), p. 21. Volkmann, "Die NS Wirtschaft unter dem 'Neuen Plan,'" Militärgeschichtlichen Forschungsamt, *Das Deutsche Reich und der Zweite Weltkrieg,* Vol. 1, p. 270.

14. Burton H. Klein, *Germany's Economic Preparations For War* (Cambridge, 1959), p. 32.

15. Maurice Williams, "German Imperialism and Austria, 1938," *Journal of Contemporary History* Vol. 14, No. 1 (January 1979): p. 144.

16. Volkmann, "Die NS Wirschaft unter dem 'Neuen Plan,'" Militärgeschichtlichen Forschungsamt, *Das Deutsche Reich und der Zweite Weltkrieg,* Vol. 1, p. 273.

17. Peter Hayes, *Industry and Ideology* (New York, 1987), p. 115.

18. Goralski and Freeburg, *Oil and War,* pp. 17–21.

19. United States Strategic Bombing Survey, "The Effects of Strategic Bombing on the German War Economy" (Washington, D.C., 31 October 1945), p. 75. (Hereafter cited as USSBS.)

20. Volkmann, "Die Wehrwirtschaft im Zeichen des Vierjahresplans," Militärgeschichtlichen Forschungsamt, *Das Deutsche Reich und der Zweite Weltkrieg,* Vol. 1, p. 283.

21. Wilhelm Deist, "Die Wehrmacht des Dritten Reich," Militärgeschichtlichen Forschungsamt, *Das Deutsche Reich und der Zweite Weltkrieg,* Vol. 1, p. 498.

22. Overy, *War and Economy in the Third Reich,* p. 178.

23. Carroll, *Design For Total War,* p. 122.

24. International Military Tribunal, Trial of the Major War Criminals (Nuremberg, 1947–1949), Document 3730–PS, Vol. XXXIII, pp. 33–37. (Hereafter cited as IMT, TTMWC, 3720–PS, Vol. XXXIII, pp. 33–37.)

25. Overy, *War and Economy in the Third Reich,* p. 95.

26. IMT, TTMWC, 420–EC, Vol. XXXVI, pp. 498–500.

27. Deist, "Die Wehrmacht des Dritten Reich," Militärgeschichtlichen Forschungsamt, *Das Deutsche Reich und der Zweite Weltkrieg,* Vol. 1, p. 499.

28. Carroll, *Design For Total War,* p. 122.

29. Alan Milward, *The German Economy at War* (London, 1965), p. 106. 30. Lothar Burchardt, "The Impact of the War Economy on the Civilian Population of Germany During the First and Second World Wars," Deist, ed., *The German Military in the Age of Total War* (Dover, 1985), p. 64.

31. Milward, *The German Economy at War,* p. 32.

32. Deist, *The Wehrmacht and German Rearmament* (London, 1981), pp. 86–101, and Overy, *War and Economy in the Third Reich,* p. 313.

33. Overy, *Why the Allies Won* (New York, 1995), p. 205.

34. Adolf Hitler, *Hitler's Secret Book* (New York, 1961), p. 155.

35. Deist, "Die Aufrüstung der Wehrmachtteile 1933–1939." Militärgeschichtlichen Forschungsamt, *Das Deustche Reich und der Zweite Weltkrieg,* Vol. 1, p. 451.

36. Deist, *The Wehrmacht and German Rearmament,* p. 71.

37. Jost Dülffer, "Determinants of German Naval Policy, 1920–1939, Deist, ed., *The German Military in the Age of Total War,* p. 163.

38. Hitler, *Hitler's Secret Book,* p. xiv.

39. Gerhard L. Weinberg, *A World at Arms* (New York, 1994), p. 28, and Overy, *War and Economy in the Third Reich,* p. 191.

40. Deist, "Die Aüfrustung der Wehrmachtteile," Militärgeschichtlichen Forschungsamt, *Das Deutsche Reich und der Zweite Weltkrieg,* Vol. 1, p. 464.

41. Wilhelm Brandt, "Stellungskrieg oder Bewegungskrieg?," *Militär Wochenblatt* Vol. 120, No. 22 (11 December 1935): p. 938.

42. Deist, "Die Aüfrustung der Wehrmachtteile," Militärgeschichtlichen Forschungsamt, *Das Deutsche Reich und der Zweite Weltkrieg*, Vol. 1, pp. 464, 472.

43. Vehicles were also ordered from large scale tractor companies such as International Harvester. Charles M. Baily, *Faint Praise* (Hamden, 1983), pp. 34, 155.

44. Overy, *Why the Allies Won*, p. 202.

45. USSBS, "Tank Industry Report," (Second ed.), (Washington, D.C., January 1947), p. 2.

46. Carroll, *Design For Total War*, p. 198.

47. Wagenführ, *Die Deutsche Industrie im Kriege, 1939–1945*, p. 59.

48. About 80% of the German Army's tank park in 1939 consisted of obsolete models. Martin van Creveld, *Fighting Power* (Westport, 1982), p. 4. For German tank development during the period 1920–1933, see James S. Corum, *The Roots of Blitzkrieg* (Lawrence, 1992), pp. 111–119.

49. General Franz Halder, *The Halder Diaries* (Washington, D.C., 1950), Vol. II, p. 83.

50. Rolf-Dieter Müller, "Von der Wirtschaftallianz zum kolonialen Ausbeutuntgskrieg," Militärgeschichtlichen Forschungsamt, *Das Deutsche Reich und der Zweite Weltkrieg*, Vol. 4, p. 185.

51. Peter Chamberlain and Hilary Doyle, *Encyclopedia of German Tanks of World War Two* (New York, 1979), pp. 6–8.

52. 11th Panzer Regiment Report to Fourth Army, 1 December 1939, NARA T-312/234/7787507, and 11th Panzer Regiment Report to Fourth Army, 12 January 1940, NARA T-312/234/7787580.

53. Guderian, *Panzer Leader*, pp. 276–283.

54. Overy, *Why the Allies Won*, p. 204.

55. Walter J. Spielberger, *Panzer IV & Its Variants* (Atglen, Pa., 1993), pp. 154–156.

56. Burkhart Müller-Hillebrand, *German Tank Maintenance in World War II* (Washington, D.C., 1954), p. 4.

57. Albert Speer, *Inside the Third Reich* (New York, 1970), p. 280.

58. Müller-Hillebrand, *German Tank Maintenance in World War II*, p. 4.

59. Speer, *Inside the Third Reich*, p. 250.

60. USSBS, "German Motor Vehicle Industry Report," (Washington, D.C., 1947), p. 5. In 1933 Daimler-Benz, with 60% of its factory capacity in use, devoted 26% of its production to the military. By 1939, working at 95% of capacity, 65% of its production was devoted to the military, and hit a peak of 93% in 1944, when Daimler-Benz reached 100% of capacity. See Bernard B. Bellon, *Mercedes in Peace and War* (New York, 1990), p. 220.

61. Vojtech Mastny, *The Czechs Under Nazi Rule* (New York, 1971), p. 66.

62. United States Army Military History Institute, Manuscript #P-103, Major General Hellmuth Reinhardt, "Utilization of Captured Material by Germany in World War II," 1953, pp. 36–37. (Hereafter cited as USAMHI, MSS #P-103.)

63. Goralski and Freeburg, *Oil and War*, p. 29.

64. Halder, *The Halder Diaries*, Vol. III, p. 54. RWM, Monthly Industrial Production Reports, November 1939–February 1940, NARA T-71/97/598402.

65. Halder, *The Halder Diaries*, Vol. III, p. 79.

66. John Terraine, *The Right of the Line* (London, 1985), p. 422. For details see Captain Peter Dickens, *Night Action* (New York, 1981), pp. 88–113.

67. John Perkins, "Coins For Conflict: Nickel and the Axis, 1933–1945," *The Historian* Vol. 55, No. 1 (Autumn 1992): p. 93.

68. Volkmann, "Die NS Wirtschaft unter dem 'Neuen Plan,'" Militärgeschichtlichen Forschungsamt, *Das Deutsche Reich und der Zweite Weltkrieg*, Vol. 1, p. 258.

69. Gerhard Schreiber, "Die politische und militärische Entwicklung im Mittelmeerraum 1939/40," Militärgeschichtlichen Forschungsamt, *Das Deutsche Reich und der Zweite Weltkrieg*, Vol. 3, p. 21.

70. Williamson Murray, *The Change in the European Balance of Power, 1938–1939* (Princeton, 1984), p. 327.

71. Goralski and Freeburg, *Oil and War*, p. 31.

72. IMT, TTMWC, 606–EC, Vol. XXXVI, pp. 580–581.

73. Maurice Pearton, *Oil and the Romanian State* (New York, 1971), p. 251.

74. Hans Umbreit, "Die Ausbeutung der besetzen Gebiete," Militärgeschichtlichen Forschungsamt, *Das Deutsche Reich und der Zweite Weltkrieg*, Vol. 5, pp. 222–223. See also IMT, TTMWC, 183–RF, Vol. XXXVIII, pp. 536–548.

75. Umbreit, "Die Ausbeutung der besetzen Gebiete," Militärgeschichtlichen Forschungsamt, *Das Deutsche Reich und der Zweite Weltkrieg*, Vol. 5, p. 224. Germany also gained some 9,000 tons of nickel, about the equivalent of a year's wartime supply for German industry. Perkins, "Coins For Conflict," p. 96.

76. Goralski and Freeburg, *Oil and War*, p. 36.

77. Quartermaster of Fourth Army, Special Order #25 For Supply, 29 June 1940, NARA T-312/121/7652686.

78. Quartermaster of Fourth Army, Special Order #30 For Rear Services, 4 July 1940, NARA T-312/121/7652590.

79. USAMHI, MSS #P-103, p. 7.

80. General Hermann Hoth, *Panzer-Operationen* (Heidelberg, 1956), p. 45. 81. War Diary of 14th Panzer Division, 31 March 1943 (Hereafter cited as KTB/14th Panzer Division, 31 March 1943), NARA T-315/657/000062.

82. This was at least parly due to the fact that of the 1,500 trucks, there were 17 different makes and 58 different models. Bernd Stegmann, "Die italienischdeutsche Kriegführung in Mittelmeer und in Nord Africa," Militärgeschichtlichen Forschungsamt, *Das Deutsche Reich und der Zweite Weltkrieg*, Vol. 3, p. 361.

83. Unless otherwise noted, the source for all charts is Müller-Hillebrand, *Das Heer, 1933–45* (Frankfurt-am-Main, 1954), Vol. II.

84. Müller, "Das Scheiten der wirtschaftlichen 'Blitzkriegstrategie,'" Militärgeschichtlichen Forschungsamt, *Das Deutsche Reich und der Zweite Weltkrieg*, Vol. 4, p. 960.

85. Second Panzer Group to Fourth Army, 26 April 1941, NARA T-313/79/ 7317771.

86. Werner Haupt, *Heeresgruppe Mitte* (Dorheim, 1968), p. 25 and Haupt, *Heeresgruppe Nord* (Bad Neuheim, 1966), p. 26.

87. Hoth, *Panzer-Operationen*, p. 45.

88. USAMHI, MSS #P-103, p. 20.

89. 11th Panzer Division Readiness Report, 16 October 1941, NARA T-315/2320/000204. Goralski and Freeburg, *Oil and War*, p. 73.

90. Müller, "Das Scheiten der wirtschaftlichen 'Blitzkriegstrategie,'" Militärgeschichtlichen Forschungsamt, Das Deutsche Reich und der Zweite Weltkrieg, Vol. 4, p. 974. RWM Monthly Industrial Production Report, December 1941, NARA T-71/97/598713.

91. Guderian, *Panzer Leader*, p. 190.

92. Halder, *The Halder Diaries*, Vol. VII, p. 133.

93. Rolf Stoves, *Die 1. Panzer Division* (Bad Neuheim, 1961), p. 302. See also 10th Panzer Division, Report on Effective Tank Strength, 21 December 1941, NARA T-315/568/001661. It should also be noted that of the Division's 25 operational tanks, 11 were obsolete Pz IIs that were soon to be taken out of service.

94. 5th Panzer Division After-Action Report on the Winter War of 1941/42 in Russia, 20 May 1942, NARA T-78/202/6145525. For details, see DiNardo, *Mechanized Juggernaut or Military Anachronism?*, pp. 48–50.

95. Steven J. Zaloga, "Technological Surprise and the Initial Period of War: The Case of the T-34 Tank in 1941," *The Journal of Slavic Military Studies* Vol. 6, No. 4 (December 1993): p. 635.

96. Halder, *The Halder Diaries*, Vol. VII, p. 212.

97. Chamberlain and Doyle, *Encyclopedia of German Tanks of World War Two*, p. 120.

98. Müller-Hillebrand, *German Tank Maintenance in World War II*, p. 25.

99. Joachim Engelmann, *Zitadelle* (Dorheim, 1982), p. 71.

100. Inspector General of Panzer Troops, Discussion Points For the Führer Conference of 3 December 1943, 3 December 1943, NARA T-78/720/000348.

101. 1st SS Panzer Regiment, LSSAH, Total Losses of Tanks, 9 May 1944, NARA T-78/720/000264.

102. Spielberger, *Panther & Its Variants* (Atglen, Pa., 1993), p. 96.

103. Memo From Guderian to Hitler to be Presented at the Führer Conference of 20 October 1943, 19 October 1943, NARA T-78/720/000394.

104. Otto Weidinger, *Division Das Reich* (Osnabrück, 1979), Vol. IV, p. 330. Aside from numbers, all SS divisions had names or titles, usually derived from German history or Nazi Party figures or symbols. The 9th SS Panzer Division, for example, had the name *Hohenstaufen*, after the early Germany medieval dynasty. A complete list of division names is in George H. Stein, *The Waffen SS* (Ithaca, 1966), pp. 296–298. For most of the war, the Army had numbered divisions with only two exceptions, the elite *Panzer Lehr* and *Gross Deutschland* Divisions. During the very late stages of the war, some newly formed panzer and panzer grenadier divisions were given names instead of numbers, such as *Feldherrnhalle, Clausewitz, Kurmark* and *Holstein.*

105. Stoves, *Die 1. Panzer Division*, p. 422, and Peter Strassner, *Europäische Freiwillige* (Osnabrück, 1968), p. 266.

106. Ernst Klink, *Das Gesetz des Handelns: Die Operation "Zitadelle"* (Stuttgart, 1966), p. 44.

107. Guderian, *Panzer Leader*, p. 311.

108. Klink, *Das Gesetz des Handelns*, p. 44.

109. Spielberger, *Panzer IV & Its Variants*, p. 148.

110. Guderian, *Panzer Leader*, p. 295.

111. Inspector General of Panzer Troops, Tank Distribution, 4 May 1943, NARA R-78/720/000479. With so many variants of the Pz III and Pz IV in service at the same time, the Germans did not refer in reports to the different versions of the same tank by letter (Pz III J, etc.). Rather, different versions of the same tank were broadly grouped according to length of the barrel of the tank's main gun. Thus, in the document cited here, for example, Pz IIIs and Pz IVs are referred to as either "short" (kurz) or "long" (lang).

112. Inspector General of Panzer Troops, Proposal For Führer Conference of 27 March 1944 (Part B), 23 March 1944, NARA T-78/720/000285. A recent work based largely on Soviet sources claims that the German tanks were immobilized by the spring mud. David M. Glantz and Jonathan House, *When Titans Clashed: How the Red Army Stopped Hitler* (Lawrence, 1995), p. 190.

113. Inspector General of Panzer Troops, Proposal For Führer Conference of 27 March 1944 (Annex 2 of Part B), 23 March 1944, NARA T-78/720/000291.

114. KTB/Army Group B, 10 July 1944, NARA T-311/1/7000801.

115. Charles Messenger, *Hitler's Gladiator* (New York, 1988), p. 134.

116. Readiness Report of 2nd Panzer Division to Inspector General of Panzer Troops, 5 July 1944, NARA T-78/718/000136.

117. Readiness Report of 8th Panzer Division to Inspector General of Panzer Troops, 16 August 1944, NARA T-78/718/000035, and Readiness Report of 23rd Panzer Division to Inspector General of Panzer Troops, 13 August 1944, NARA T-78/718/000082.

118. Readiness Report of 1st Panzer Division to Inspector General of Panzer Troops, 1 August 1944, NARA T-78/718/000004.

119. Inspector General of Panzer Troops, Notice of Decision of Field Marshal Keitel, 10 May 1944, NARA T078/720/000255.

120. Weinberg, *A World at Arms*, p. 400.

121. Readiness Report of 23rd Panzer Division to Inspector General of Panzer Troops, 13 August 1944, NARA T-78/718/000082.

122. Readiness Report of Panzer Lehr Division to Inspector General of Panzer Troops, 16 June 1944, NARA T-78/718/000373.

123. Readiness Report of 21st Panzer Division to Inspector General of Panzer Troops, 7 August 1944, NARA T-78/718/000077.

124. Readiness Report of 12th Panzer Division to Inspector General of Panzer Troops, 5 August 1944, NARA T-78/718/000044.

125. Readiness Report of 7th Panzer Division to Inspector General of Panzer Troops, 12 August 1944, NARA T-78/718/000030. See also Readiness Report of 16th Panzer Division to Inspector General of Panzer Troops, 1 August 1944, NARA T-78/718/000062, and Readiness Report of 23rd Panzer Division to Inspector General of Panzer Troops, 13 August 1944, NARA T-78/718/000082.

126. Army Group B Quartermaster Report, 29 July 1944, NARA T-311/1/ 7000828.

127. Creveld, *Supplying War* (London, 1977), p. 222.

128. USSBS, "German Motor Vehicle Industry Report," p. 17.

129. Readiness Report of 20th Panzer Division to Inspector General of Panzer Troops, 9 August 1944, NARA T-78/718/000073. See also Readiness Report of 13th Panzer Division to Inspector General of Pazner Troops, 8 August 1944, NARA T-78/718/000052.

130. Percy Schram, ed., *Kriegstagebuch des Oberkommando der Wehrmacht* (Frankfurt-am-Main, 1963), Vol. I, p. 218. (Hereafter cited as KTB/OKW.)

131. USSBS, "The Effects of Strategic Bombing on the German War Economy," p. 74. For details see Creveld, *Supplying War*, pp. 142–180.

132. Göring to Frank, 23 July 1942, NARA T-77/632/1825214.

133. Milward, *The German Economy at War*, p. 119.

134. Pearton, *Oil and the Romanian State*, pp. 261–262.

135. Transcript of Conference of German and Romanian Petroleum Experts Held in Bucharest, 16 March 1944, NARA T-77/11/722532.

136. *Wi Rü Amt*, Oil Situation in Romania and Hungary, 15 May 1944, NARA T-77/489/1653445.

137. Goralski and Freeburg, *Oil and War*, p. 269.

138. Supplement to Memorandum From Army Group B Quartermaster Staff to Operations Section, 29 May 1944, NARA T-311/1/70000636.

139. RWM, Oil Security Plan, 1 August 1944, NARA T-71/110/613020.

140. RWM, Report on Oil in Austria 1944–45, 6 March 1945, NARA T-71/7/399141.

141. RWM. Report on Oil in Serbia and Croatia, 8 June 1944, NARA T-71/1/394530.

142. *Wi Rü Amt*, Oil Situation in Romania and Hungary, 15 May 1944, NARA T-77/489/1653445.

143. Rolf Hinze, *Der Zusammenbruch der Heeresgruppe Mitte im Osten, 1944* (Stuttgart, 1980), p. 20.

144. Readiness Report of 11th Panzer Division to Inspector General of Panzer Troops, 5 August 1944, NARA T-78/718/000040.

145. OKH Organization Section, Study For Armaments in 1944, 26 January 1944, NARA T-78/414/6382118.

146. The Germans did field some 48 panzer and panzer grenadier divisions by the end of July 1944, but that is only if one includes SS and Luftwaffe divisions as well as Army divisions. OKH, Summary of Large Units of the Army, Waffen SS, and Parachute Troops as of 30 July 1944, 31 July 1944, NARA T-78/413/ 6381074.

147. F. M. von Senger and Etterlin, *Die Panzergrenadiere* (Munich, 1961), p. 203.

148. Field Marshal Erich von Manstein, *Aus Einem Soldatenleben, 1887–1939* (Bonn, 1958), p. 244.

149. Inspector General of Panzer Troops, Note For Führer Conference, 5 September 1943, NARA T-78/720/000442. See also Memo From Guderian to Hitler to be Presented at the Führer Conference of 20 October 1943, 19 October 1943, NARA T-78/720/000394.

150. Spielberger, *Panzer III & Its Variants* (Atglen, Pa., 1993), p. 80, and Guderian, *Panzer Leader*, p. 298.

151. See for example Inspector General of Panzer Troops, Note For Führer Conference, 5 September 1943, NARA T-781720/000442 and Excerpt From Draft of Gen. d. Inf./Gen. d. Art. No. 4800/43(Ib) Booklet "Instructions For the Action of Assault Guns in Cooperation With Infantry," c.1943, NARA T-78/720/000445.

152. Inspector General of Panzer Troops, Führer Conference of 10 May 1944, 10 May 1944, NARA T-78/720/000257.

153. Richard Ogorkiewicz, *Armor* (New York, 1960), p. 79.

154. Special Report From Army Group B Quartermaster to OKH on Production and Allocation of Italian Vehicles, 17 November 1943, NARA T-311/5/7005087.

155. Readiness Report of 21st Panzer Division to Inspector General of Panzer Troops, 7 August 1944, NARA T-78/718/000077.

156. Senger and Etterlin, *Die Panzergrenadiere*, pp. 207–208.

157. U.S. Army, "ETHINT 10: Peiper in the Ardennes," Donald Detwiler ed., *World War II German Military Studies* (New York, 1979), Vol. 2, p. 1.

158. Inspector General of Panzer Troops, Proposal For Panzer Division, 9 March 1945, NARA T-78/720/000090.

159. It is difficult to estimate the number of horses authorized for a panzer division, but about 1,000 would seem a reasonable guess. DiNardo, *Mechanized Juggernaut or Military Anachronism?*, p. 103.

160. Readiness Report of 1st Panzer Division to Inspector General of Panzer Troops, 5 July 1944, NARA T-78/718/000132.

161. Murray, *Luftwaffe* (Baltimore, 1985), p. 317.

162. Quartermaster enclosures to KTB/Seventh Army, 14 June 1944, NARA T-312/1571/000660.

163. Manstein, *Aus Einem Soldatenleben*, p. 241.

CHAPTER TWO

1. Wilhelm Prüller, *Diary of a German Soldier* (London, 1963), p. 111.

2. 20th Panzer Division, Combat Lessons From the Recent Defensive Battles, 8 April 1944, NARA T-311/224/000196.

3. Guderian, "Kraftfahrtruppen," *Militärwissenschaftliche Rundschau*, Vol. 1, No. 1, (December 1935): p. 74.

4. Reichs-Kredit-Gesellschaft, *Treibstoffwirtschaft in der Welt und in Deutschland*, c.1939, NARA T-84/51/1332658.

5. KTB/OKW, Vol. I, p. 66.

6. Gerhard Rempel, *Hitler's Children: The Hitler Youth and the SS* (Chapel Hill, 1989), p. 41.

7. IMT, TTMWC, 2654–PS, Vol. XXXI, pp. 59–63.

8. Rempel, *Hitler's Children*, p. 22.

9. Kenneth Macksey, *Guderian: Panzer General* (London, 1975), p. 61.

10. Murray, *Luftwaffe*, p. 6.

11. Müller-Hillebrand, *German Tank Maintenance in World War II*, pp. 41–42.

12. Creveld, *Fighting Power*, p. 67. Horst Fuchs Richardson and Dennis E. Showalter eds., *Sieg Heil: War Letters of Tank Gunner Klaus Fuchs, 1937–1941* (Hamden, 1987), pp. 41–12.

13. All of the 1st Panzer Division's units were located in Wehrkreis IX. Stoves, *Die 1. Panzer Division*, pp. 24–25.

14. Georg Tessin, *Verbände und Truppen der deutschen Wehrmacht und Waffen SS im Zweiten Weltkrieg* (Osnabrück, 1977), Vol. II, p. 105.

15. This has been challenged somewhat by Omer Bartov in *Hitler's Army*, which discounts this and emphasizes the influence of Nazi ideology instead. While I would agree with Bartov to an extent on this, I believe he overstates his case. Omer Bartov, *Hitler's Army* (New York, 1991), pp. 29–58.

16. Creveld, *Fighting Power*, p. 44. See also Stephen G. Fritz, *Frontsoldaten: The German Soldier in World War II* (Lexington, 1995), pp. 157, 235.

17. Creveld, *Fighting Power*, p. 99. Report on 7th Panzer Division convalescent Home at Sables d'Olonne, 18 November 1942, NARA T-315/2315/001194.

18. Fritz, *Frontsoldaten*, p. 179.

19. Inspector General of Panzer Troops, Memo For Führer Conference on 5 March 1944 (Annex 1), 4 March 1944, NARA T-78/720/000306.

20. Readiness Report of 2nd Panzer Division to Inspector General of Panzer Troops, 5 July 1944, NARA T-78/718/000136.

21. Prüller, *Diary of a German Soldier*, p. 149.

22. William Craig, *Enemy at the Gates* (New York, 1973), p. 167.

23. *Gross Deutschland* Panzer Grenadier Division, Organization, Command and Training of Subordinate Units of Panzer Grenadiers, 24 May 1943, NARA T-84/308/000466.

24. 20th Panzer Division, Combat Lessons From the Recent Defensive Battles, 8 April 1944, NARA T-311/224/000196.

25. Readiness Report of Panzer Lehr Division to Inspector General of Panzer Troops, 6 August 1944, NARA T-78/718/000099.

26. Bernd Wegner, "Der Krieg gegen die Sowjetunion 1942/43," Militärgeschichtlichen Forschungsamt, *Das Deutsche Reich und der Zweite Weltkrieg*, Vol., 6, p. 1005.

27. Richard Müller, *The German Air War in Russia* (Baltimore, 1992), p. 99.

28. KTB/OKW, Vol. II, p. 319.

29. Liddell-Hart, ed., *The Rommel Papers* (New York, 1953), p. 266.

30. Hans von Luck, *Panzer Commander* (New York, 1989), p. 132.

31. Bryan Perrett, *Knights of the Black Cross* (New York, 1986), p. 240.

32. KTB/14th Panzer Division, 23 March 1943, NARA T-315/657/000065.

33. KTB/14th Panzer Division, 20 June 1943, NARA T-315/657/000022.
34. KTB/24th Panzer Division, March-June 1943, NARA T-315/805/000005.
35. Bernhard Kroener, "Squaring the Circle. Blitzkrieg Strategy and the Manpower Shortage," Deist, ed., *The German Military in the Age of Total War*, 287.
36. Halder, *The Halder Diaries*, Vol. III, p. 46. For a fresh look at the role of women in the work force, see Overy, *War and Economy in the Third Reich*, pp. 303–311. Some companies, however, did prefer to use foreign slave labor as opposed to women. At Daimler-Benz' main production facility at Unterturkheim, for example, as late as 1944 only 460 German women were employed there. Bellon, *Mercedes in Peace and War*, p. 250.
37. Murray, *Luftwaffe*, p. 116. "Der Dicke" was a derogatory term often applied to Göring by his detractors. Literally translated, it means "the fat one," or perhaps more idiomatically, "fatty."
38. Seaton, *The German Army, 1933–45* (New York, 1982), p. 202.
39. Murray, *Luftwaffe*, p. 116.
40. OKH, Summary of Large Units of the Army. Waffen SS and the Parachute Troops as of 30 July 1944, 31 July 1944, NARA T-78/413/6381074.
41. Wegner, "'My Honor is My Loyalty.' The SS as a Military Factor in Hitler's Germany," Deist, ed., *The German Military in the Age of Total War*, p. 228.
42. IMT, TTMWC, 2567–PS, Vol. XXX, p. 602.
43. Charles W. Sydnor, *Soldiers of Destruction* (Princeton, 1977), p. 258.
44. Rempel, *Hitler's Children*, p. 208.
45. IMT, TTMWC, 3245–PS, Vol. XXXII, pp. 55–56.
46. Wegner, "'My Honor Is My Loyalty.' The SS as a Military Factor in Hitler's Germany," Deist, ed., *The German Military in the Age of Total War*, p. 225. Peter Padfield, *Himmler* (New York, 1990), p. 316.
47. General Paul Hausser, *Soldaten Wie Anders Auch* (Osnabrück, 1966), p. 122.
48. Jürgen Förster, "Freiwillige fur den Kreuzzug Europas gegen den Bolschewismus," Militärgeschichtlichen Forschungsamt, *Das Deutsche Reich und der Zweite Weltkrieg*, Vol. 4, p. 908.

49. Ibid., p. 910.
50. Strassner, *Europäische Freiwillige*, p. 27.
51. IMT, TTMWC, 926–RF, Vol. XXXVIII, p. 694 and IMT, TTMWC, 056–UK, Vol. XXXIX, p. 117.
52. Stein, *The Waffen SS*, p. 246.
53. KTB/OKW, Vol. III, pp. 159, 234.
54. Leo J. Daugherty III, "The Volksdeutsche and Hitler's War," *The Journal of Slavic Military Studies*, Vol. 8, No. 2, (June 1995): p. 302.
55. Weidinger, *Division Das Reich*, Vol. V, p. 130.
56. Sydnor, *Soldiers of Destruction*, p. 205.
57. James Weingartner, *Hitler's Guard* (Carbondale, 1974), p. 94.
58. H. W. Koch, *The Hitler Youth* (New York, 1976), p. 244. Inspector General of Panzer Troops, Führer Conference of 10 May 1944, Observations From the Visit to the Area of OB West 28 April-9 May 1944, 10 May 1944, NARA T-78/720/000248.
59. When the German Army employed men well past military age, they were collected in battalions by ailment. Hence, a "stomach" battalion was composed of men with stomach ailments.
60. Corum, *The Roots of Blitzkrieg*, pp. 69–70.
61. David N. Spires, *Image and Reality* (Westport, 1984), p. 6.
62. Creveld, *Fighting Power*, p. 123.
63. Stein, *The Waffen SS*, p. 10.
64. Rudolf Absolon, *Wehrgesetz and Wehrdienst* (Boppardam-Rhein, 1960), p. 226.
65. James Lucas, *War on the Eastern Front, 1941–1945* (New York, 1976), p. 151.
66. Creveld, *Fighting Power*, p. 141.
67. 20th Panzer Division, Combat Lessons From the Recent Defensive Battles, 8 April 1944, NARA T-311/224/000196.
68. Readiness Report of 2nd Panzer Division to Inspector General of Panzer Troops, 5 July 1944, NARA T-78/718/000136.
69. Creveld, *Fighting Power*, pp. 127–162.
70. John Brown Sloan, *Draftee Division* (Lexington, 1986), p. 175.
71. The airborne divisions were used rather sparingly, and in operations where their participation was not absolutely necessary to the operation's success, with the exception of Market-Garden. In short, given the number of operations they were

in and the manpower and resources they consumed, the Allied airborne divisions were wasteful in the extreme.

CHAPTER THREE

1. A number of armies have used this motto in the past, and the Germans were no exception. I SS Panzer Corps, *Training for Corps Staff and Units of I SS Panzer Corps*, 9 November 1943, NARA T-354/603/000576.
2. Commander Panzer Group West, *Current Training Directive No. 4*, 24 March 1944, NARA T-84/308/000494.
3. Richard D. Challener, *The French Theory of the Nation in Arms, 1866–1939* (New York, 1965), p. 73.
4. Eleanor Hancock, "Ernst Röhm and the Experience of World War I," *The Journal of Military History*, Vol. 60. No. 1 (January 1996): p. 40.
5. Koch, *The Hitler Youth*, p. 238, and Rempel, *Hitler's Children*, pp. 178–179.
6. Gordon Craig, *Germany, 1866–1945*, p. 587. For a different interpretation, see Hancock, "Ernst Röhm and the Experience of World War I," pp. 58–60.
7. Herman Rauschning, *Hitler Speaks* (London, 1939), p. 154.
8. IMT, TTMWC, 1949–PS, Vol. XXVIII, p. 583.
9. IMT, TTMWC, 3993–PS, Vol. XXXIII, p. 594.
10. David Irving, *The Trail of the Fox* (New York, 1978), p. 37, and Rempel, *Hitler's Children*, p. 180.
11. IMT, TTMWC, 1992–PS, Vol. XXIX, p. 189.
12. Lieutenant Hans Sturm, born in 1920, served in a Hitler Youth Naval Unit where he showed promise as a signalman. After his father refused permission for him to go on a world cruise as it would interfere with his engineering career, Sturm wound up in the Army as a Lieutenant in the 253rd Infantry Division, winning the Knight's Cross in Russia in 1942. Gordon Williamson, *Infantry Aces of the Reich* (London, 1991), pp. 59–65.
13. Fritz, *Frontsoldaten*, p. 15.
14. Creveld, *Fighting Power*, p. 72.
15. American Military Attaché Report on Basic Principles concerning the Education of the German Soldier, 30 January

1937, Military Intelligence Division Report #2016–1279. (Hereafter cited as MID 2016–1279.)

16. Fritz, *Frontsoldaten*, pp. 12–13.
17. American Military Attaché Report on Divisional Anti-Tank Battalion, 8 February 1937, MID 2016–1236/10.
18. Ibid.
19. Creveld, *Fighting Power*, p. 29.
20. MID 2016–1236/10.
21. American Military Attaché Report on German Army Motor Transport Combat School, 20 May 1936, MID 2277–B-43/1.
22. American Military Attaché Report on the Preparation of Training Schedules, 3 February 1941, MID 2016–1004/57.
23. Brown, *Draftee Division*, p. 48.
24. Richard W. Stewart, "The 'Red Bull' Division: The Training and Initial Engagements of the 34th Infantry Division, 1941–1943," *Army History*, No. 25, (Winter 1993): p. 3.
25. Donald E. Houston, *Hell on Wheels* (San Rafael, 1977), pp. 38–39.
26. American Military Attaché Report on Training Devices of a German Anti-Tank Company, 31 October 1936, MID 2016–1236/8.
27. Inspector General of Panzer Troops, "Anti-Tank Combat of All Weapons," 4 December 1944, NARA T-78/620/000520.
28. MID 2016–1236/8.
29. Creveld, *Fighting Power*, p. 68.
30. MID 2016–1236/10.
31. MID 2016–1236/8.
32. Army Group Three Report on Action of Eighth Army in March 1938 in Austria's Reunion With Germany, 18 July 1938, NARA T-79/14/000447.
33. Halder, *The Halder Diaries*, Vol. II, p. 22.
34. Guderian, *Panzer Leader*, pp. 71–72.
35. After-Action Report of the 7th Panzer Division (Formerly the 2nd Light Division), 19 October 1939, NARA T-315/436/000480.
36. Murray, *The Change in the European Balance of Power, 1938–1939*, pp. 338–339.

37. Training Memorandum From 10th Panzer Division Commanding General to Division Units, 31 October 1939, NARA T-315/558/000812.

38. Report of 10th Panzer Division on Training, 14 December 1939, NARA T-315/558/000733.

39. Sydnor, *Soldiers of Destruction*, p. 81, and Rudolf Lehmann, *Die Leibstandarte* (Osnabrück, 1977), Vol. I, p. 210.

40. Murray, "The German Response to Victory in Poland: A Case Study in Professionalism," *Armed Forces and Society*, Vol. 7, No. 2, (Winter 1981): 294.

41. American Military Attaché Report on German Leadership, 1940, 18 November 1940, MID 2016–1329/3.

42. Weidinger, *Division Das Reich*, Vol. II, p. 23.

43. Stoves, *Die 1. Panzer Division*, p. 415.

44. OKH Training Directive, 22 November 1940, NARA T-315/584/000216.

45. OKH Instructions For Training, 7 October 1940, NARA T-315/664/000028.

46. Training Instructions From 21st Panzer Division Staff to Division Units, 9 May 1942, NARA T-315/768/000562.

47. Lieutenant Braun, "Combat Experiences of Lieutenant Braun of 25th Panzer Regiment in the French Campaign," c. July 1940, Part of the "Rommel Collection," NARA T-84/277/000010.

48. Fritz, *Frontsoldaten*, pp. 39, 141.

49. See for example Inspector General of Panzer Troops, Bulletin to Panzer Units No. 1, 15 July 1943, NARA T-84/308/000494, and Commander, Panzer Group West, Current Training Directive No. 4, 24 March 1944, NARA T-84/308/000494.

50. American Military Attaché Report on Visit to German Armor School at Wunsdorf, 4 October 1940, 11 October 1940, MID 2277–B-43/5.

51. German Army Tank School, Instructions For Company Commander of a Panzer Company in Combat, July 1943, NARA T-84/308/000461.

52. *Gross Deutschland* Panzer Grenadier Division, Organization, Command and Training of Subordinate Panzer Grenadiers, 24 May 1943, NARA T-84/308/ 000466.

53. Commander, Panzer Group West, Current Training Directive No. 4, 24 March 1944, NARA T-84/308/000494.

54. 116th Panzer Division, Combat Lessons From Normandy, 15 July 1944, NARA T-84/309/000773.

55. Corum, "The Luftwaffe's Army Support Doctrine, 1918–1941," *The Journal of Military History*, Vol. 59, No. 1 (January 1995): p. 60.

56. For Richthofen's activities in Spain, see Richthofen Papers, File N/671/2, Bundesarchiv-Militararchiv, Freiburg-im-Breisgau, Germany. (Hereafter cited as BA-MA, N/671/2.)

57. After-Action Report of 4th Light Division, 22 October 1939, NARA T-315/230/000307.

58. OKH Instructions For Training, 7 October 1940, NARA T-315/664/000028.

59. Corum, "The Luftwaffe's Army Support Doctrine, 1918–1941," p. 76.

60. Weidinger, *Division Das Reich*, Vol. IV, p. 150.

61. Sajer's novel is of great interest because there are very few first hand accounts of actual German Army training. It is evident, however, that aside from personal experience, Sajer also spoke to a number of veterans to capture the flavor of the German Army at war on the eastern front. Erich Maria Remarque used the same technique before writing *All Quiet on the Western Front*. The *Gross Deutschland* was one of the few elite Army units with a name instead of a number. Some works based on Soviet sources consistently misidentify the *Gross Deutschland* as an SS unit. See for example John Erickson, *The Road to Berlin* (Boulder, 1983), p. 64.

62. Guy Sajer, *The Forgotten Soldier* (New York, 1964), pp. 199–202.

63. USAMHI, MSS #D-138, SS Major General Klaus Mölhoff, "The SS Panzergrenadier School," 1947, pp. 6–7.

64. SS Headquarters, Bulletin For Anti-Tank Combat of All Weapons No. 2, 8 June 1944, NARA T-354/116/3750069.

65. Training Instructions From I SS Panzer Corps to Subordinate Units, 9 November 1943, NARA T-354/603/000576.

66. USAMHI, MSS #D-110, Major General Helmuth Bachelin, "Officer Procurement of the German Army During World War II," 1947, p. 19.

67. Hausser, *Soldaten Wie Andere Auch*, p. 46.

68. USAMHI, MSS #D-178, SS Major General Wemer Dörffler, "SS Officer Procurement," 1947, p. 5.

69. USAMHI, MSS #D-138, pp. 2–4.

70. Richard Schülze-Kossens, *Militärischer Führernachwuchs der Waffen SS: die Junkerschulen* (Osnabrüch, 1982), p. 16.

71. Lehmann, *Die Leibstandarte*, Vol. I, p. 82.

72. Fritz, *Frontsoldaten*, pp. 194–195.

73. Wehrkreis VII Order, 14 August 1935, NARA T-79/37/000876.

74. SS Main Office, Office For Officer Training, Standard Description of SS Junker and Reserve Officer Candidate Classes, 20 March 1942, NARA T-175/35/000414.

75. Wegner, *Hitlers Politische Soldaten: Die Waffen SS, 1933–1945* (Paderborn, 1982), pp. 150–151.

76. Arden Bucholz, *Moltke, Schlieffen and Prussian War Planning* (Oxford, 1991), pp. 75–76.

77. German Army, *Richtlinien für die Führung der Panzer-division*, 1 June 1938, p. 7.

78. OKH Training Section, Order Provided For General Staff Officer Training, 15 February 1940, NARA T-311/47/705771, and OKH Training Section to Army Group C and XIV Corps, 17 February 1940, NARA T-311/47/7057769.

79. USAMHI, MSS #B-036, General Hasso von Manteuffel, "Mobile and Panzer Troops," 1945, pp. 11–12.

80. Brown, *Draftee Division*, pp. 99.

81. Creveld, *Fighting Power*, pp. 89–90.

82. Brown, *Draftee Division*, p. 17.

83. Daniel J. Hughes, "Schlichting, Schlieffen, and the Prussian Theory of War in 1914," *The Journal of Military History*, Vol. 59, No. 2, (April 1995): p. 261.

84. John A. English, *On Infantry* (New York, 1981), p. 49.

85. American Military Attaché Report on German Anti-Tank Units and Tactics, 15 October 1935, MID 2016–1236/1.

86. German Army, *Truppenführung*, 1933, p. 1. The same exact sentence was used for the 1936 edition of the manual. It is based on Carl von Clausewitz, *On War* (Michael Howard and Peter Paret eds. and trans.), (Princeton, 1976), p. 148.

87. *Gross Deutschland* Panzer Grenadier Division, Organization, Command and Training of Subordinate Units of Panzer Grenadiers, 24 May 1943, NARA T-84/308/000466.

88. German Army Tank School, Instructions For Company Commander of a Tank Company in Combat, July 1943, NARA T-84/308/000461.

89. Creveld, *Fighting Power*, p. 73.

90. Wegner, *Hitlers Politische Soldaten*, p. 158.

91. Readiness Report of 11th Panzer Division to Inspector General of Panzer Troops, 5 August 1944, NARA T-78/718/000040.

92. Readiness Report of Panzer Lehr Division to Inspector General of Panzer Troops, 6 August 1944, NARA T-78/718/000099.

93. 20th Panzer Division, Combat Lessons From the Recent Defensive Battles, 8 April 1944, NARA T-311/224/000196.

94. USAMHI, MSS #C-024, SS Major General Fritz Kramer, "I SS Panzer Corps in the West in 1944," p. 30.

95. Memo From Army Group Don to Fourth Panzer Army and Attack Group Hollidt on Field NCO School For Mobile Troops at Rembertow, 18 December 1942, NARA T-311/269/000533.

96. Army Group B to All Subordinate Army Commands, 2 October 1944, NARA T-311/4/7003371.

97. See for example Training Instructions From 21st Panzer Division Staff to Division Units, 9 May 1942, NARA T-315/768/000562 and *Gross Deutschland* Panzer Grenadier Division, Organization, Command and Training of Subordinate Units and Panzer Grenadiers, 24 May 1943, NARA T-84/308/000466.

CHAPTER FOUR

1. A somewhat shorter version of this chapter has been published as an article in *War in History* Vol. 3, No. 4 (November 1996): pp. 384–397.

2. Guderian, *Panzer Leader*, p. 20.

3. Inspector General of Panzer Troops, Memo by Guderian on Operational Reserves to be Presented to Hitler at the Führer

Conference of 27 March 1944, 23 March 1944, NARA
T-78/720/000279.

4. Guderian, *Panzer Leader*, p. 20.

5. See for example Bryan Perrett, *A History of Blitzkrieg* (New
York, 1983), p. 65, Robert H. Larson, *The British Army and the
Theory of Armored Warfare, 1918–1940* (Newark, 1984), pp.
226–227, Murray, *The Change in the European Balance of Power,
1938–1939*, p. 34, and Brian Bond, "Liddell-Hart and the German Generals," *Military Affairs*, Vol. 41, No. 1 (February
1977): p.17.

6. John J. Mearsheimer, *Liddell-Hart and the Weight of History*
(Ithaca, 1988), pp. 164–217.

7. Macksey, *Guderian: Panzer General*, p. 41. One might want to
compare Guderian, *Erinnerungen eines Soldaten* (Heidelberg,
1951), p. 15, and Guderian, *Panzer Leader*, p. 20.

8. Dermot Bradley, *Generaloberst Heinz Guderian und die Entstehungsgeschichte des modernen Blitzkrieg* (Osnabrück, 1978), p.
152.

9. See for example Unsigned, "Kampfwagenausbildung in Russland," *Militär Wochenblatt* Vol. 111, No. 13 (4 October 1926):
pp. 444–445, Unsigned, "Kampfwagen and Kavallerie," *Militär
Wochenblatt* Vol. 111, No. 38 (11 April 1927): pp. 1405–1406
and Unsigned, "Die Panzerwaffe in Fernost," *Mititär Wochenblatt* Vol. 117, No. 13 (4 October 1932): pp. 417–423.

10. Guderian, "Kraftfahrtruppen," *Militärwissenschaftliche Rundschau* Vol. 1, No. 1 (December 1935): p. 69.

11. Guderian, "Die Panzertruppen und ihr Zusammenwirken mit
den anderen Waffen," *Militärwissenschaftliche Rundschau* Vol. 1,
No. 5 (March 1936): pp. 615, 619.

12. Guderian, *Achtung-Panzer!* (Stuttgart, 1937), p. 214.

13. See for example Lieutenant Colonel Hoffmeister, "Der
Angriff von Panzerkraften im Zusammenwirken mit Infan-
terie einer nicht mot. Division und deren Artillerie," c.1936,
NARA T-79/48/000592.

14. American Military Attaché Report on Military Reading List
for German Officers, MID 2016–1004/56.

15. Larson, *The British Army and the Theory of Armored Warfare,
1918–1940*, p. 62.

16. Corum, *Roots of Blitzkrieg*, pp. 122–123.

17. Creveld, *Supplying War*, p. 126.
18. For details see Norman Stone, *The Eastern Front, 1914–1917* (New York, 1975), pp. 264–281.
19. Seaton, *The German Army, 1933–45*, pp. 61–62.
20. Corum, *The Roots of Blitzkrieg*, pp. 132–133. For a somewhat different view of Seeckt, see Spires, *Image and Reality*, p. 107.
21. American Military Attache Report on German Army Maneuvers of September 1930, 19 December 1930, MID 2016–1095/9.
22. Corum, *The Roots of Blitzkrieg*, pp. 191, 194. For a long time, not much has been known about the Russo-German collaboration, especially on the Soviet side. That should change, however, as more and more material comes out of the Russian archives since the collapse of the Soviet Union. For some older scholarship, see John Erickson, *The Soviet High Command* (London, 1962), pp. 144–163. See also Glantz and House, *When Titans Clashed*, p. 7.
23. Bruce I. Gudmundsson, *Stormtroop Tactics: Innovation in the German Army, 1914–1918* (Westport, 1989), pp. 91–104. See also Paddy Griffith, *Forward into Battle* (New York, 1981), p. 80.
24. For some eyewitness accounts, see Field Marshal Erwin Rommel, *Infantry Attacks* (Vienna, 1979), pp. 201–276. See Gudmundsson, *Stormtroop Tactics*, pp. 107–170, and Captain Timothy T. Lupfer, *The Dynamics of Doctrine: The Changes in German Tactical Doctrine During the First World War* (Fort Leavenworth, 1981).
25. German Army, *Command and Combat of the Combined Arms* (Fort Leavenworth, 1925), p. 118. This is the U.S. Army's translation of the 1921 German field service regulation, *Führung und Gefecht.*
26. Ibid., pp. 99–100.
27. Hans von Seeckt, *Thoughts of a Soldier* (London, 1930), pp. 84–85, and Corum, *The Roots of Blitzkrieg*, p. 32.
28. See for example Unsigned, "Kraftradfahrer als fechtende Truppe," Lieutenant General Konstantine von Altrock ed., *Taktik and Truppenführung in kriegsgeschichtlichen Beispielen* (Berlin, 1929), pp. 160–163.
29. Major General J.F.C. Fuller, *Armored Warfare* (Harrisburg, 1943), p. 115. This was actually the 1943 annotated edition of

his most famous work on tanks, *Lectures on FSR III* (London, 1932). The only changes from the 1932 edition were the annotations. See also Fritz Heigl, *Taschenbuch der Tanks* (Munich, 1927), p. 161.

30. German Army, *Command and Combat of the Combined Arms*, pp. 198–199.

31. First Lieutenant Uto Gallwitz, "Beiträge zur Kampfwagenab-wehr," *Militär Wochenblatt* Vol. 111, No. 9 (4 September 1926): p. 295.

32. Gallwitz, "Infanteriegeschutz und Kampfwagenabwehr," *Militär Wochenblatt* Vol. 111, No. 14 (11 October 1926): p. 486.

33. Major Ernst Volckheim, *Die deutschen Kampfwagen im Weltkrieg* (Berlin, 1923), pp. 100–102.

34. Guderian, *Panzer Leader*, p. 24, and Corum, *The Roots of Blitzkrieg*, pp. 134–136.

35. After-Action Report on Experimental Exercises of a Panzer Division at the Drill Ground at Munster in August 1935, 24 December 1935, NARA T-79/52/000750.

36. Fuller, *Armored Warfare*, p. 18.

37. Liddell-Hart, *Paris or the Future of War* (New York, 1925), p. 73.

38. Liddell-Hart, *The Remaking of Modern Armies* (London, 1927), pp. 57, 60. Liddell-Hart later laid the failure of the British to develop a balanced combined arms armored division on the influence of Fuller. Liddell-Hart, "The Development of Armored Infantry—Tank Marines," (No Date). B. H. Liddell-Hart Unpublished Papers, Special Collections, Kreitzberg Library, Norwich University, Northfield, Vermont. (Hereafter cited as Liddell-Hart Papers, NU.) It is worth pointing out here Liddell-Hart's writings on tanks dated mostly from the 1920s. After 1930 he became much more interested in broader matters such as imperial defense.

39. After-Action Report on Experimental Exercises of a Panzer Division at the Drill Ground at Munster in August 1935, 24 December 1935, NARA T-79/52/000750.

40. Guderian, "Die Panzertruppen und ihr Zusammenwirken mit den anderen Waffen," p. 618, Unsigned, "Gedanken uber das Zusammenwirken der Pioniere mit den anderen Waffen," *Militär Wochenblatt* Vol. 121, No. 4 (25 July 1936): p. 172 and

German Army, *Richtlinien für die Führung der Panzerdivision*, 1 June 1938, p. 27.

41. John Keegan, *Six Armies in Normandy* (New York, 1982), p. 172.

42. Disappointed with the performance of the Pioneer Regiment in the Seven Years' War, Frederick the Great converted them to regular infantry. Thereafter, most engineering tasks were accomplished by regular troops, while under the command of engineer officers. Christopher Duffy, *The Army of Frederick the Great* (New York, 1974), p. 123.

43. See for example Fuller, *On Future Warfare* (London, 1928), p. 333.

44. Corum, *The Roots of Blitzkrieg*, p. 153.

45. Field Marshal Wilhelm Ritter von Leeb, *Die Abwehr* (Berlin, 1938), p. 92.

46. Guderian, "Die Panzertruppen und ihr Zusammenwirken mit den anderen Waffen," p. 622.

47. American Military Attaché Report on Combined Efforts of Tanks with Planes, 14 November 1934, MID 2016–1200/1.

48. Murray, Luftwaffe, p. 17. See also Muller, *The German Air War in Russia*, p. 18, and Corum, "The Luftwaffe's Army Support Doctrine, 1918–1939," pp. 65–68.

49. German Army, *Richtlinien für die Führung der Panzerdivision*, 1 June 1938, p. 20.

50. Ibid., p. 24.

51. Guderian, *Panzer Leader*, p. 21.

52. Even the excellent German "semi-official" history gives the impression that Guderian was the sole creator of German armor doctrine. Other theorists receive no mention at all. Deist, "Die Aufrüstung der Wehrmacht," *Das Deutsche Reich und der Zweite Weltkrieg*, Vol. 1, pp. 426–427. A much more balanced assessment is given in Walter Nehring, *Die Geschichte der Deutschen Panzerwaffe, 1916 bis 1945* (Berlin, 1969), pp. 87–93.

53. Corum, *The Roots of Blitzkrieg*, pp. 127, 193.

54. Volckheim, *Der Kampfwagen in der heutigen Kriegführung*, (Berlin, 1924), pp. 28–30.

55. Nehring, "Panzerabwehr," *Militärwissenschaftliche Rundschau* Vol. 1, No. 2 (March 1936): pp. 187–194.

56. General Ludwig Ritter von Eimannsberger, Der Kampfwagenkrieg (Berlin, 1938), p. 125.

57. Guderian, "Schnell Truppen einst und jetzt," *Militärwissenschaftliche Rundschau* Vol. 4, No. 2 (March 1939): p. 241. See also General Georg Reinicke, "Kampfwagenabwher," *Militär Wochenblatt* Vol. 120, No. 39 (20 April 1936), p. 1753 and Lieutenant Colonel Walter Spannenkrebs, *Angriff mit Kampfwagen* (Berlin, 1939), p. 50.

58. Halder to Guderian, 10 October 1940, NARA T-313/78/7316921.

59. Guderian, *Panzer Leader*, p. 32.

60. Klaus-Jürgen Müller, *Armee, Politik und Gesellschaft in Deutschland, 1933–1945* (Paderborn, 1979), p. 89.

61. Murray, "German Army Doctrine 1918–1939, and the Post-1945 Theory of 'Blitzkrieg Strategy,'" Carole Fink, Isabel V. Hull and MacGregor Knox eds., *German Nationalism and the European Response, 1890–1945* (Norman, 1985), p. 80.

62. Müller, *General Ludwig Beck* (Boppard-am-Rhein, 1980), pp. 209–210.

63. This sentence begins the 1921 and 1925 editions of *Führung und Gefecht* and the 1933 and 1936 editions of *Truppenführung*. See also Clausewitz, *On War*, p. 148.

64. Gudmundsson, *Stormtroop Tactics*, p. 172.

65. Generalfeldmarschal Helmuth, Graf von Moltke, *Ausgewählte Werke*, F. von Schmerfeld ed., (Berlin, 1925), Vol. I, p. 296.

66. Hughes, "Schlichting, Schlieffen, and the Prussian Theory of War," pp. 261–262.

67. Rommel, *Infantry Attacks*, pp. 235–249. One may notice that I have refrained from the use of the term *Auftragstaktik*. That is because if one peruses the German literature with any care, the term almost never appears. Its overuse to the point of corruption by the United States Army in the 1980s became in the words of one recent author, "something of an embarrassment." Antulio J. Echevarria II, "Moltke and the German Military Tradition: His Theories and Legacies," *Parameters* Vol. XXVI, No. 1 (Spring 1996): pp. 96, 99. During the period of the U.S. Army's ardent embrace of German terms, a cautionary note was sounded in Hughes, "Abuses of German Military

History," *Military Review* Vol. LCVI, No. 12 (December 1986): pp. 66–76.

68. German Army, *Richtlinien für die Führung der Panzerdivision,* 1 June 1938, p. 24.

69. After-Action Report of the 10th Panzer Division on the Polish Campaign, 15 October 1939, NARA T-315/548/000817. See also Critique of Polish Campaign by 3rd Panzer Regiment, 20 January 1940, NARA T-78/379/6344436.

70. Guderian, "Truppen auf Kraftwagen und Fliegerabwehr," *Militär Wochenblatt* Vol. 109, No. 12 (25 September 1924): p. 306.

71. German Army, *Vorläufige Anweisungen für Ausbildungen von Panzereinheiten,* Teil I, *Formen und Bewegungen,* 15 December 1937, p. 7.

72. American Military Attaché Report on German Anti-Tank Units and Tactics, 15 October 1935, MID 2016–1236/1. It is worth pointing out that rigid or "schematic" thinking was one of the major faults the Germans found in the armies of their Axis allies. DiNardo, "The Dysfunctional Coalition: The Axis Powers and the Eastern Front in World War II," *The Journal of Military History* Vol. 60, No. 4 (October 1996): p. 722.

73. U.S. Army, "ETHINT 13: Geyr von Schweppenburg in Normandy," Donald S. Detwiler ed., *World War II German Military Studies* (New York, 1979), Vol. 2, p. 3. It might be added that this opinion was completely in contrast to wartime documents signed by Geyr. See for example Commander Panzer Group West, Current Training Directive No. 4, 24 March 1944, NARA T-84/308/000494.

74. After-Action Report of 4th Light Division, 22 October 1939, NARA T-315/230/000307.

75. After-Action Report of the 10th Panzer Division on the Polish Campaign, 15 October 1939, NARA T-315/558/000817.

76. After-Action Report of 6th Panzer Division in France, 18 July 1940, NARA T-311/49/7061270.

77. Müller, *The German Air War in Russia,* p. 22.

78. German Army, *Richtlinien für Führung und Einsatz der Panzer-Division,* 3 December 1940, p. 10.

79. Liddell-Hart ed., *The Rommel Papers* (New York, 1953), p. 19. Another good first-hand description by a member of the 7th Panzer division is an undated account (probably written in

the summer of 1940) by a Lieutenant Braun, "Combat Experiences of Lieutenant Braun of 25th Panzer Regiment in the French Campaign," c. July 1940, Part of the "Rommel Collection," NARA T-84/277/000010.

80. German Army, *Richtlinien für Führung und Einsatz der Panzer-Division*, 3 December 1940, p. 7.

81. Heigl, *Taschenbuch der Tanks*, p. 161 and Volckheim, *Der Kampfwagen in der heutigen Kriegführung*, p. 6.

82. Corelli Barnett, *The Desert Generals* (New and Enlarged Edition), (Bloomington, 1982), pp. 74–76.

83. Nehring, "Panzerabwehr," p. 200.

84. Third Panzer Army, "Experiences of the Winter Campaign, 1943–1944," 9 March 1944, NARA T-78/620/000379. See also Commander XLVIII Panzer Corps, Lessons From the Offensive and Defensive Battles in the Zhitomir Berdichev Area From 15 November 1943–21 January 1944, 26 January 1944, NARA T-311/224/000212.

85. Carlo D'Este, *Decision in Normandy* (New York, 1983), p. 377.

86. Major Hans Wagner, "Gedanken über Kampfwagenabwehr," *Militär Wochenblatt* Vol. 113, No. 1 (4 July 1928): p. 10.

87. American Military Attaché Report on German Anti-Tank Units and Tactics, 15 October 1935, MID 2016–1236/1.

88. This was a luxury that the other Axis armies normally did not enjoy. Romanian anti-tank guns, for example, were drawn by horses, something that German observers felt detracted from their performance. LIV Corps to Eleventh Army, Estimate of Attached Romanian Units, 26 August 1941, NARA T-312/354/7934935.

89. Report of Instruction by a Staff Panzer Officer to Army General Staff, 16 January 1944, NARA T-312/239/7794428 and SS Headquarters, Bulletin For Anti-Tank Combat of All Weapons No. 1, 20 May 1944. NARA T-354/116/3750063.

90. See for examples After-Action Report of 6th Panzer Division in France, 18 July 1940, NARA T-311/49/7061270, Commander XLVIII Panzer Corps, Lessons From the Offensive and Defensive Battles in the Zhitomir-Berdichev Area From 15 November 1943–21 January 1944, 26 January 1944, NARA T-311/224/000212, Third Panzer Army, Experiences of the Winter Campaign, 1943–1944, 8 March 1944, NARA

T-78/620/000379 and SS Headquarters, Bulletin For Anti-Tank Combat of All Weapons No. 1, 20 May 1944, NARA T-354/116/3750063.

91. Guderian to Hitler, Memorandum For Führer Conference of 20 October 1943, 19 October 1943, NARA T-78/720/000394.

92. Inspector General of Panzer Troops, Notice of Führer Decision, 31 May 1944, NATA T-78/720/000231.

93. Inspector General of Panzer Troops, Memorandum For Führer Conference, 5 September 1943, NARA T-78/720/000442.

94. German Army, *Richtlinien für die Führung der Panzerdivision*, 1 June 1938, p. 7, and 20th Panzer Division, Combat Lessons From the Recent Defensive Battles, 8 April 1944, NARA T-311/224/000196.

95. Guderian to Hitler, Memorandum to be Presented at Führer Conference of 20 October 1943, 19 October 1943, NARA T-78/720/000394.

96. Guderian, *Panzer Leader*, pp. 25–26.

97. General Max von Poseck, "Kavallerie von einst und jetzt," *Militär Wochenblatt* Vol. 118, No. 43 (18 May 1934): p. 1467.

98. Murray, *The Change in the European Balance of Power, 1938–1939*, p. 35.

99. Unsigned, "Zusammenwirken von Panzerkraftwagen mit Kavallerie," *Militär Wochenblatt* Vol. 115, No. 33 (4 March 1931): p. 1283.

100. Guderian, "Schnell Truppen einst und jetzt," p. 242.

101. After-Action Report of the 7th Panzer Division (Formerly the 2nd Light Division), 19 October 1939, NARA T-315/436/000480.

102. 1st Cavalry Division, Activity Report For the Period 8 November 1941 to 29 April 1942, 29 April 1942, NARA T-315/83/000214. Both the Germans and the Soviets employed mounted troops on the eastern front during the war, where they were useful for operations in heavily forested or swampy terrain. See DiNardo, *Mechanized Juggernaut or Military Anachronism?* pp. 79–88.

103. Guderian, *Panzer Leader*, p. 30.

104. Nehring, *Die Geschichte der Deutschen Panzerwaffe, 1916 bis 1945*, p. 78.

105. Liddell-Hart, *The Remaking of Modern Armies*, pp. 88, 111.

106. See for example Major George A. Higgins, "German and U.S. Operational Art: A Contrast in Maneuver," *Military Review* Vol. LXV, No. 10 (October 1985): p. 23.

107. Clausewitz, *On War*, p. 227.

108. Hughes ed., *Moltke on the Art of War: Selected Writings* (Novato, 1993), p. 176 and Jehuda L. Wallach, *The Dogma of the Battle of Annihilation* (Westport, 1986), p. 218. See also Bucholz, *Moltke, Schlieffen and Prussian War Planning*, p. 156.

109. General Erich Ludendorff, *Tannenberg: Geschichtliche Wahrheit uber die Schlacht* (Munich, 1939), p. 142. See also General Hans Knoerzer, "Hannibal und Hindenburg, ein zeitgemasser Vergleich," *Militär Wochenblatt* Vol. 106, No. 13 (24 September 1921): pp. 265–268 and Dennis E. Showalter, *Tannenberg: Clash of Empires* (Hamden, 1991), p. 351.

110. For a challenge to the strategy of annihilation see Dr. Gunther Grundel, "Die Krise des Vernichtungsgedankens in der neuzeitlichen Kriegführung," *Militär Wochenblatt* Vol. 117, No. 7 (18 August 1932): pp. 209–212. For its reaffirmation, see Colonel Heinrich Ritter von Fuchtbauer, "Der Vernichtungsgedanke—entscheidend auch in der neuzeitlichen Kriegführung!" *Militär Wochenblatt* Vol. 117, No. 10 (11 September 1932): pp. 318–320.

111. Larry H. Addington, *The Blitzkrieg Era and the German General Staff* (New Brunswick, 1971), p. 216. For details on the problems facing the horsedrawn units in Russian, see DiNardo. *Mechanized Juggernaut or Military Anachronism?* pp. 35–54.

112. Inspector General of Panzer Troops, Memorandum on Operational Reserves to be Presented at Führer Conference of 27 March 1944 (Part A), 23 March 1944, NARA T-78/720/000279 and Order From Führer Headquarters, April 1944, NATA R-78/720/000265.

113. See for example Murray, "German Army Doctrine, 1918–1939, and the Post-1945 Theory of 'Blitzkrieg Strategy,'" p. 93 and the badly flawed Barry R. Posen, *The Sources of Military Doctrine* (Ithaca, 1984), p. 41.

114. Colonel Count Schack, "Deutsche Marz-Offensiv 1918 and Mai-Offensiv 1940," *Deutsche Wehr* Vol. 43, No. 29 (19 July 1940): p. 421.

CHAPTER FIVE

1. Guderian, "Die Panzertruppen und ihr Zusammenwirken mit den anderen Waffen," p. 625.
2. See organizational diagram in the records of Wehrkreis VII, NARA T-79/32/000814.
3. Compare organizational diagram in NARA T-79/32/000814 and Guderian, *Panzer Leader*, p. 518.
4. Guderian, *Panzer Leader*, p. 518.
5. Compare organizational diagram in NARA T-79/32/000814 with Annex 1 of German Army, Richtlinien für die Führung der Panzerdivision, 1 June 1938, 39.
6. Robert M. Kennedy, *The German Campaign in Poland* (Washington, 1956), pp. 28–31.
7. Senger and Etterlin, *Die Panzergrenadiere*, pp. 69–70.
8. Halder, *The Halder Diaries*, Vol. II, p. 22.
9. After-Action Report of the 7th Panzer Division (Formerly the 2nd Light Division), 19 October 1939, NARA T-315/436/000480, and Stoves, *Die 1. Panzer Division*, p. 76. See also Critique of Polish Campaign by 3rd Panzer Regiment, 22 January 1940, NARA T-78/379/6344436.
10. Guderian, "Schnell Truppen einst und jetzt," p. 242.
11. After-Action Report of the 7th Panzer Division (Formerly the 2nd Light Division), 19 October 1939, NARA T-315/436/000480 and Halder, *The Halder Diaries*, Vol. III, p. 83.
12. After-Action Report of the 4th Light Division, 22 October 1939, NARA T-315/230/000307.
13. General Baron Hasso von Manteuffel, *Die 7. Panzer Division im Zweiten Weltkrieg* (Ürdingen-am-Rhein, 1965), p. 22.
14. Tessin, *Verbände und Truppen der deutschen Wehrmacht und Waffen SS im Zweiten Weltkrieg, 1939–1945*, Vol. I, p. 161.
15. Müller-Hillebrand, *Das Heer, 1933–45*, Vol. II, p. 143.
16. Halder, *The Halder Diaries*, Vol. III, pp. 82–83.
17. Jeffrey A. Gunsberg, "The Battle of the Belgian Plain, 12–14 May 1940: The First Great Tank Battle," *The Journal of Military History*, Vol. 56, No. 2, (April 1992): p.210.
18. Müller-Hillebrand, *Das Heer, 1933–45*, Vol. II, pp. 141–143.
19. After-Action Report of the 6th Panzer Division in France, 18 July 1940, NARA T-311/49/7061270.

20. Hans Umbreit, "Der Kampf um die Vormachtstellung in Westeuropa," Militärgeschichtlichen Forschungsamt, *Das Deutsche Reich und der Zweite Weltkrieg,* Vol. 2, p. 307.

21. Rudolf Steiger, *Panzertaktik im Spiegel deutscher Kriegstagebucher, 1939–1942* (Freibrug-im-Breisgau, 1973), p. 18 and Stoves, *Die 1. Panzer Division,* p. 167.

22. Klink, "Die Militärische Konzeption des Krieges gegen die Sowjetunion," Militärgeschichtlichen Forschungsamt, *Das Deutsche Reich und der Zweite Weltkrieg,* Vol. 4, p. 262.

23. Tessin, *Verbände und Truppen der deutschen Wehrmacht und Waffen SS im Zweiten Weltkrieg, 1939–1945,* Vol. I, pp. 161–162.

24. OKH Chief of Armaments and Commander of the Replacement Army, Reorganization of Infantry Divisions into Panzer Divisions and Infantry Divisions (Mot.), 26 September 1940, NARA T-313/78/7316871.

25. OKH Chief of Armaments and Commander of the Replacement Army, Replenishment and Refitting of Panzer and Motorized Divisions, 18 July 1940, NARA T-311/48/7059866 and Stoves, *Die 1. Panzer Division,* p. 175.

26. KTB/11th Panzer Division, 1 October 1940, NARA T-315/584/000017.

27. OKH Chief of Armaments and Commander of the Replacement Army, Reorganization of Infantry Divisions into Panzer Divisions and Infantry Divisions (Mot.), 26 September 1940, NARA T-313/78/7316871.

28. Organizational Diagram of 11th Panzer Division, 20 May 1941, NARA T-315/2320/000243.

29. Müller, "Von der Wirtschaftallianz zum kolonialen Ausbeutungskrieg," Militärgeschichtlichen Forschungsamt, *Das Deutsche Reich und der Zweite Weltkrieg,* Vol. 4, pp. 186–187.

30. KTB/6th Panzer Division, 22 June 1941, NARA T-315/322/000857.

31. Organizational Diagram of 20th Panzer Division, 2 October 1940, NARA T-315/741/000764.

32. Guderian, *Panzer Leader,* pp. 138–139.

33. Liddell-Hart, *The German Generals Talk,* p. 96.

34. Nehring, *Die Geschichte der Deutsche Panzerwaffe, 1916 bis 1945,* pp. 126–130.

35. Guderian, *Panzer Leader,* p. 198.

36. OKH Report on Combat Strength of the Eastern Army, 6 November 1941, NARA T-78/335/6291878.

37. 11th Panzer Division Readiness Report, 19 December 1941, NARA T-315/2320/000215.

38. Department of the Army Pamphlet 20–201, Military Improvisation During the Russian Campaign (Washington D.C., 1951), p. 4.

39. 5th Panzer Division, After-Action Report on the Winter War of 1941/42 in Russia, 20 May 1942, NARA T-78/202/6145525. See also DiNardo, *Mechanized Juggernaut or Military Anachronism?* p. 48.

40. Tessin, *Verbände und Truppen der deutschen Wehrmacht und Waffen SS im Zweiten Weltkrieg, 1939–1945*, Vol. I, p. 174.

41. Stoves, *Die 1. Panzer Division*, p. 342.

42. Ibid., p. 413.

43. Inspector General of Panzer Troops, Tank Distribution, 4 May 1943, NARA T-78/720/000479.

44. Organizational diagram of 11th Panzer Division, May 1943, NARA T-315/657/000125. The Panthers were delivered largely in May and June 1943. Inspector General of Panzer Troops, Tank Deliveries, 3 May 1943, NARA T-78/720/000460.

45. 2nd Panzer Division Report, 1 July 1943, NARA T-315/96/000840. The authorized organization for the 1943 panzer division, formalized in September 1943, is in Senger and Etterlin, *Die Panzergrenadiere*, p. 203.

46. Guderian, *Panzer Leader*, p. 311.

47. Appendix to Wehrkreis VII Order #2594, Supplementary Instructions on the Arming of SS Units, NARA T-79/38/000017.

48. Lehman, *Die Leibstandarte*, Vol. I, p. 149.

49. Weidinger, *Division Das Reich*, Vol. I, p. 120.

50. Appendix to Wehrkreis VII Order #2272, 25 April 1939, NARA T-79/38/000030.

51. Lehmann, *Die Leibstandarte*, Vol. I, pp. 210–218. For the SS *Totenkopf*, see Sydnor, *Soldiers of Destruction*, pp. 64–86.

52. Strassner, *Europäische Freiwillige*, p. 23.

53. Stein, *The Waffen SS*, p. 203.

54. Sydnor, *Soldiers of Destruction*, p. 254.

55. Strassner, *Europäische Freiwillige*, p. 116. See also Weidinger, *Division Das Reich*, Vol. III, p. 440 and Sydnor, *Soldiers of Destruction*, p. 257.

56. Lehmann, *Die Leibstandarte*, Vol. II, p. 325 and Sydnor, *Soldiers of Destruction*, p. 255.

57. The SS *Leibstandarte Adolf Hitler* Division, for example, was designated 1st SS Panzer Division (*Adolf Hitler*) on 22 October 1943. KTB/I SS Panzer Corps, 28 October 1943, NARA T-354/603/000538. The 2nd SS Panzer Division (*Das Reich*), according to its historian only received its designation in June 1944. Weidinger, *Division Das Reich*, Vol. V, p. 138.

58. Report of 2nd Panzer Division to Inspector General of Panzer Troops, 1 July 1944, NARA T-78/718/000137.

59. Report of 1st SS Panzer Division to Inspector General of Panzer Troops, 1 June 1944, NARA T-78/719/000064.

60. For the origins of the Panzer Lehr Division, see Franz Kurowski, *Die Panzer Lehr Division* (Bad Neuheim, 1964), p. 7 and Helmut Ritgen, *Die Geschichte der Panzer Lehr Division im Westen, 1944–1945* (Stuttgart, 1979), pp. 11–26. Compare Readiness Report of Panzer Lehr Division to Inspector General of Panzer Troops, 16 June 1944, NARA T-78/718/000373 with 2nd Panzer Division, Report on New Organization to Panzer Group West, 3 May 1944, NARA T-78/718/000420. A good comparison of the Panzer Lehr's organization with that of American and British armored divisions can be found in Ritgen, *Die Geschichte der Panzer Lehr Division im Westen, 1944–1945*, p. 343.

61. Report of 1st SS Panzer Division to Inspector General of Panzer Troops, 1 June 1944, NARA T-78/719/000064.

62. Report of 12th Panzer Division to Inspector General of Panzer Troops, 1 June 1944, NARA T-78/719/000099.

63. German Army, *Vorläufge Richtlinien für Führung und Kampf der Panzer-Brigade, 26 July 1944*, p. 9. USAMHI, MSS #B-251, General Horst Stumpff, "106th Panzer Brigade," 1947, p. 5.

64. Readiness Report of 10th Panzer Brigade to Inspector General of Panzer Troops, 16 August 1944, NARA T-78/718/000014.

65. USAMHI, MSS #B-251, p. 6.

66. German Army, *Vorläufige Richtlinien Für Führung und Kampf der Panzer-Brigade*, 26 July 1944, p. 1.

67. USAMHI, MSS #A-871, Lieutenant General Edgar Feuchtinger, "21st Panzer Division in Combat Against American Troops in France and Germany," 1947, p. 15.

68. Memorandum From Guderian to Hitler to be Presented at the Führer Conference of 20 October 1943, 19 October 1943, NARA T-78/720/000394,

69. Seaton, *The German Army, 1933–45*, p. 242.

70. Inspector General of Panzer Troops, Proposal For Panzer Division, 9 March 1945, NARA T-78/720/000090. See also Senger und Etterlin, *Die Panzergrenadiere*, pp. 226–228. Although no firm numbers are available, it would seem likely that a 1945 panzer division probably needed about 1,000 horses if not more. DiNardo, *Mechanized Juggernaut or Military Anachronism?* p. 103.

71. Basic Organizations and Special Organizations of SS Units, 15 February 1945, NARA T-354/116/3750050.

72. German Army, *Richtlinien Für die Führung der Panzerdivision*, 1 June 1938, p. 39.

73. As far as I could discover, the Army issued no revised editions of this manual after the edition dated 3 December 1940.

74. German Army, *Richtlinien für die Führung der Panzerdivision*, 1 June 1938, p. 21.

75. 11th Panzer Division Report, 26 June 1941, NARA T-315/2320/000200.

76. Spielberger, Panzer III & Its Variants, p. 58. The Pz IV also had a similar mix of shells. "Combat Experiences of Lieutenant Braun of 25th Panzer Regiment in the French Campaign," c. July 1940, Part of the "Rommel Collection," NARA T-84/277/000010.

77. Report of Kampfgruppe Baumgart to XL Panzer Corps, 15 November 1941, NARA T-315/568/000531.

78. Stoves, *Die 1. Panzer Division*, pp. 444–445 and USAMHI, MSS #D-079, Lieutenant General Rudolf von Wagenfels, "Advance and Breakthrough of the 6th Panzer Division on 15–16 July 1944," 1947, p. 4.

79. John Keegan, *Six Armies in Normandy* (New York, 1982), pp. 205–210 and Luck, *Panzer Commander*, pp. 148–161.

80. Ritgen, *Die Geschichte der Panzer Lehr Division im Westen, 1944–1945*, p. 181.

81. Charles MacDonald, *A Time For Trumpets* (New York, 1985), p. 198.

82. Weidinger, *Division Das Reich*, Vol. 1, p. 262.

83. Guderian, *Panzer Leader*, pp. 242–244.

84. Organization of Korpsgruppe Fischer as of 9 January 1943, NARA T-315/570/000318.

85. USAMHI, MSS #B-036, pp. 11–12.

86. Kent Roberts Greenfield, et al., *The Organization of Ground Combat Troops* (Washington, 1947), p. 323.

87. Russell F. Weigley, *Eisenhower's Lieutenants* (Bloomington, 1981), p. 19.

88. Brown, *Draftee Division*, p. 99.

89. Greenfield, *The Organization of Ground Combat Troops*, pp. 334–335. 90. For details on the creation of these units, see Barrie Pitt, *The Crucible of War* (London, 1980), pp. 69–70.

91. Glantz and House, *When Titans Clashed*, p. 176.

92. Creveld, *Fighting Power*, pp. 57–58.

93. KTB/10th Panzer Division, 20 December 1941, NARA T-315/568/001638.

94. Michael D. Doubler, *Closing With the Enemy* (Lawrence, 1994), p. 40.

95. KTB/14th Panzer Division, 31 March 1943, NARA T-315/657/000062.

96. KTB/14th Panzer Division, 8 April 1943, NARA T-315/657/000058. 97. Manstein, *Aus Einem Soldatenleben, 1887–1939*, p. 241.

98. Seaton, *The German Army, 1933–45*, p. 135.

99. Guderian, *Panzer Leader*, p. 99.

100. Ibid., p. 120.

101. Müller, "Von der Wirtschaftallianz zum kolonialen Ausbeu-tungskrieg," Militärgeschichtlichen Forschungsamt, *Das Deutsche Reich und der Zweite Weltkrieg*, Vol. 4, pp. 186–187.

102. Bryan I. Fugate, *Operation Barbarossa* (Novato, 1994), p. 110.

103. KTB/OKW, Vol. I, p. 681.

104. KTB/OKW, Vol. II, p. 187.

105. Quartermaster of the First Panzer Group, Lessons in the Area of Supply From the Serbian Campaign, 22 April 1941, NARA T-313/2/7226128.

106. Liddell-Hart, *History of the Second World War*, p. 251 and Hoth, *Panzer-Operationen*, p. 40.

107. Haupt, *Heeresgruppe Mitte*, p. 160.

108. For a good account of the DLM in action, see Gunsberg, "The Battle of the Belgian Plain 12–14 May 1940: The First Great Tank Battle," pp. 207–244. See also Senger und Etterlin, *Die Panzergrenadiere*, p. 154.

109. L. F. Ellis, *The War in France and Flanders, 1939–1940* (London, 1953), pp. 367–371.

110. In the later years of the war this was due to a serious manpower shortage in Britain. For details see Carlo D'Este, *Decision in Normandy* (New York, 1983), pp. 253–270.

111. Zaloga and James Grandsen, *Soviet Tanks and Combat Vehicles of World War II* (London, 1984), pp. 146–149.

112. Figure adapted from Organizational Diagram, NARA T-79/32/000814.

113. After-Action Report on the Experimental Exercises of a Panzer Division at the Munster Training Area in August 1935, 24 December 1935, NARA T-79/ 52/000750.

114. Organizational Diagram, NARA T-79/32/000814.

115. Figure adapted from German Army. *Richtlinien für die Führung der Panzerdivision*, 1 June 1938, p. 39.

116. Figure adapted from War Organization Diagram of 14th Panzer Division, 4 June 1941, NARA T-315/195/000851.

117. Organizational Diagram, 11th Panzer Division, 20 May 1941, NARA T-315/2320/000243.

118. Figure adapted from Sydnor, *Soldiers of Destruction*, p. 45.

119. Figure adapted from Senger und Etterlin, *Die Panzergrenadiere*, pp. 218–220.

120. The 1st Panzer Division, for example, by 1 August 1944 was authorized 78 Pz IVs and 73 Panthers, while the 3rd Panzer was authorized 93 Pz IVs and 99 Panthers. Compare Readiness Report of 1st Panzer Division to Inspector General of Panzer Troops, 1 August 1944, NARA T-78/718/000004 and Readiness Report of 3rd Panzer Division to Inspector General of Panzer Troops, 1 August 1944, NARA T-78/718/000009.

121. Readiness Report of 1st SS Panzer Division to Inspector General of Panzer Troops, 1 July 1944, NARA T-78/719/000015.

CHAPTER SIX

1. German Army, *Richtlinien für die Führung der Panzerdivision,* 1 June 1938, p. 7.

2. For a preliminary examination see DiNardo and Austin Bay, "Horse Drawn Transport in the German Army," *Journal of Contemporary History,* Vol. 23, No. 1, (January 1988): pp. 129–142. A more extensive treatment of the subject is DiNardo, *Mechanized Juggernaut or Military Anachronism?*

3. Liddell-Hart, *The Remaking of Modern Armies,* p. 88.

4. Manstein, *Aus Einem Soldatenleben, 1887–1939,* p. 241.

5. Creveld, *Supplying War,* p. 145.

6. Addington, *The Blitzkrieg Era and the German General Staff,* p. 216.

7. Brandt, "Stellungskrieg oder Bewegungskrieg?", p. 938.

8. Weinberg, *A World at Arms,* p. 28.

9. Goralski and Freeburg, *Oil and War,* p. 338.

10. Müller-Hillebrand, *German Tank Maintenance in World War II,* pp. 41–42.

11. MacDonald, *A Time for Trumpets,* p. 45.

12. USAMHI, MSS #B-036, pp. 11–12.

13. Brown, *Draftee Division,* p. 99.

14. House, *Towards Combined Arms Warfare* (Fort Leavenworth, 1984), p. 50

15. John B. Wilson, "Influences on U.S. Army Divisional Organization in theTwentieth Century," *Army History,* No. 39, (Fall 1996): p. 5.

Bibliography

DOCUMENTARY SOURCES

International Military Tribunal, *Trial of the Major War Criminals.* 42 Vols.

Nuremberg: Government, 1947–1949.

National Archives Microfiled German Records

Series T-71: Ministry of Economics

Series T-77: Armed Forces High Command (OKW)

Series T-78: Army High Command (OKH)

Series T-79: Military Districts (*Wehrkreise*)

Series T-84: Miscellaneous Documents

Series T-175: Office of the Reichsführer SS

Series T-311: Army Groups

Series T-312: Field Armies

Series T-313: Panzer Groups and Armies

Series T-314: Corps

Series T-315: Divisions

Series T-354: SS Units

Schramm, Percy Ernst, ed. *Kriegstagebuch des Oberkommando der Wehrmacht.* 4 Vols. Frankfurt-am-Main: Bernard Graefe für Wehrwesen, 1963.

United States Military Attaché Reports From Germany, 1920–1941. National Archives, Washington, D.C.

UNPUBLISHED PAPERS

B. H. Liddell-Hart Papers, Norwich University, Northfield, Vermont.

Wolfram Freiherr von Richthofen Papers, Bundesarchiv-Militärarchiv, Freiburg-im-Breisgau, Germany.

UNPUBLISHED MANUSCRIPTS

United States Army Military History Institute. MSS #A-871, Lieutenant General Edgar Feuchtinger. "21st Panzer Division in Combat Against American Troops in France and Germany." 1947.

———. MSS #A-904, General Freiherr Heinrich von Lüttwitz. "2nd Panzer Division in the Normandy Campaign 26 July–6 September 1944." 1945.

———. MSS #B-036, General Hasso von Manteuffel. "Mobile and Panzer Troops." 1945.

———. MSS #B-058, Major General H. Voightsberger. "116th Panzer Division (21 August–19 September 1944)." 1946.

———. MSS #B-251, General Horst Stumpff. "106th Panzer Brigade." 1947.

———. MSS #B-418, General Dietrich von Choltitz. "LXXXIV Corps (18 June–15 July 1944)." March 1947.

———. MSS #B-466, General Leo Freiherr Geyr von Schweppenberg. "Panzer Group West (Mid 1943–5 July 1944)." 1947.

United States Army Military History Institute. MSS #B-716, Percy Schramm. "Wehrmacht Losses." No Date.

———. MSS #B-847, Field Marshal Gerd von Rundstedt. "Notes on the 1939 Polish Campaign." 1954.

———. MSS #C-024, SS Major General Fritz Krämer. "I SS Panzer Corps in the West in 1944." 1948.

———. MSS #C-033, Lieutenant General Oldwig von Natzmer. "Commitment of German Armor 1943–1945." 1948.

———. MSS #D-079, Lieutenant General Rudolf von Wagenfels. "Advance and Breakthrough of the 6th Panzer Division on 15–16 July 1944." 1947.

———. MSS #D-110, Major General Helmuth Bachelin. "Officer Procurement in the German Army in World War II." 1947.

———. MSS #D-138, SS Major General Klaus Mölhoff. "The SS Panzergrenadier School." 1947.

———. MSS #D-178, SS Major General Wemer Dörffler. "Officer Procurement in the Waffen SS." 1947.

———. MSS #P-059, General Burkhardt Müller-Hillebrand. "Tank Losses." 1950.

———. MSS #P-080, General Hellmuth Reinhardt. "The Training of Senior Officers." 1951.

United States Army Military History Institute. MSS #P-103, General Hellmuth Reinhardt, et al. "Utilization of Captured Material by Germany in World War II." 1953.

————. MSS #P-190, General Rudolf Hoffman and Major General Alfred Toppe. "Consumption and Attrition Rates Attendant to the Operations of German Army Group Center in Russia 22 June–31 December 1941." 1953.

————. MSS #T-11, Colonel General Heinz Guderian. "Flank Defense in Far-Reaching Operations." 1948.

————. MSS #T-26, General Theodore Busse. "The Zitadelle Offensive 1943." 1947.

GERMAN ARMY FIELD MANUALS

German Army, *Führung and Gefecht.* 1921.

————. *Truppenführung.* 1933.

————. *Truppenführung,* 1936.

————. *Richtlinien für die Führung der Panzerdivision.* 1 June 1938.

————. *Richtlinien für Führung und Einsatz der Panzer-Division.* 3 December 1940.

————. *Vorläufige Anweisungen für die Ausbildung von Panzereinheiten.* Teil I: *Formen und Bewegungen.* 15 December 1937.

————. *Vorläufige Richtlinien für Führung und Kampf der Panzer-Brigade.* 26 July 1944.

PUBLISHED WORKS

Absolon, Rudolf. *Wehrgesetz und Wehrdienst, 1935–1945.* Boppard-am-Rhein: Harald Boldt Verlag, 1960.

Addington, Larry. *The Blitzkrieg Era and the German General Staff.* New Brunswick: Rutgers University Press, 1971.

Altrock, Lieutenant General Constantine von, ed. *Taktik und Truppenführung in kriegsgeschichtlichen Beispielen.* Berlin: E. S. Mittler und Sohn, 1929.

Baentsch, Lieutenant Colonel Alfred. "Der Motor in der Durchbruchschlacht." *Militärwissenschaftliche Rundschau.* Vol. 3, No. 1, (January 1938): pp. 83–99.

————. "Der Infanterie in der durchbruchschlacht." *Militärwissenschaftliche Rundschau.* Vol. 3, No. 4, (July 1938): pp. 506–524.

Baily, Charles. *Faint Praise.* Hamden: Archon Books, 1983.

Balck, General Hermann. *Ordnung in Chaos.* Osnabrück: Biblio Verlag, 1980.

Baldwin, Hanson W. *Battles Lost and Won.* New York: Harper and Row Publishers, Inc., 1966.

Barnett, Correlli. *The Desert Generals.* (Rev. Ed.) Bloomington: Indiana University Press, 1982.

———, ed. *Hitler's Generals.* New York: Grove Weidenfeld and Nicolson Ltd., 1989.

Bartov, Omer. *The Eastern Front, 1942–45: German Troops and the Barbarization of Warfare.* London: The Macmillan Press Ltd., 1985.

———. *Hitler's Army.* New York: Oxford University Press, 1991.

Bartz, Major E. "Kriegsflugzeuge, ihre Aufgaben und Leistung." *Militärwissenschaftliche Rundschau.* Vol. 1, No. 2, (March 1936): pp. 204–229.

Beaumont, Roger A. "On the Wehrmacht Mystique." *Military Review.* Vol. LXVI, No. 7, (July 1986): pp. 44–56.

Beck, Earl R. *Under the Bombs.* Lexington: The University Press of Kentucky, 1986.

Bellon, Bernard P. *Mercedes in Peace and War.* New York: Columbia University Press, 1990.

Bidwell, Shelford and Graham, Dominick. *Firepower.* London: George Allen and Unwin, 1982.

Blau, George E. *The German Campaign in Russia—Planning and Operations (1940–1942).* Washington: Department of the Army, 1955.

———. *The German Campaigns in the Balkans.* Washington: Department of the Army, 1953.

Blumentritt, General Gunther. *Von Rundstedt: The Soldier and the Man.* London: Oldhams Press, Ltd., 1952.

Bond, Brian. "Liddell-Hart and the German Generals." *Military Affairs.* Vol. 41, No. 1, (February 1977): pp. 16–20.

Boog, Horst. *Die deutsche Luftwaffenführung, 1935-1945.* Stuttgart: Deutsche-Verlags Anstalt, 1982.

Bradley, Dermot. *Generaloberst Heinz Guderian und die Entstehungsgeschichte des modernen Blitzkrieges.* Osnabrück: Biblio Verlag, 1980.

———. *Walther Wenck.* Osnabrück: Biblio Verlag, 1981.

Brandt, Wilhelm. "Aufklarungskrafte und Schnelle Truppen." *Militär Wochenblatt.* Vol. 119, No. 40, (25 April 1935): pp. 1586–1588.

————. "Stellungskrieg oder Bewegungskrieg?" *Militär Wochenblatt.* Vol. 120, No. 22, (11 December 1935): pp. 937–939.

————. "Wie soll das Fussvolk den Tankangriff begleiten." *Militär Wochenblatt.* Vol. 120, No. 6, (11 August 1935): pp. 237–238.

————. "Die Kunstige Entwicklung der Panzerfahrzeuge." *Militär Wochenblatt.* Vol. 120, No. 14, (11 October 1935): pp. 574–575.

Brett-Smith, Richard. *Hitler's Generals.* San Rafael: Presidio Press, 1977.

Brown, John Sloan. *Draftee Division.* Lexington: The University Press of Kentucky, 1986.

Brownlow, Donald Grey. *Panzer Baron.* North Quincy: The Christopher Publishing House, 1975.

Buchner, Alex. *Ostfront 1944: The German Defensive Battles on the Eastern Front 1944.* West Chester, Pa.: Schiffer Publishing, 1991.

Bucholz, Arden. *Moltke, Schlieffen and Prussian War Planning.* Oxford: Berg Publishers, 1991.

Carell, Paul. *Scorched Earth.* Boston: Little, Brown and Company, 1970.

Carroll, Berenice A. *Design For Total War.* The Hague: Mouton and Company, 1968.

Carsten, F. L. *The Reichswehr and Politics.* London: Oxford University Press, 1966.

Carver, Field Marshal Lord Michael. *The Apostles of Mobility.* New York: Holmes and Meier Publishers, Inc., 1979.

Challener, Richard D. *The French Theory of the Nation in Arms, 1866–1939.* New York: Russell and Russell Inc., 1965.

Chamberlain, Peter and Doyle, Hilary. *Encyclopedia of German Tanks of World War Two.* New York: Arco Publishing Company, Inc., 1987.

Citino, Robert M. *The Evolution of Blitzkrieg Tactics.* Westport: Greenwood Press, 1987.

Clark, Alan. *Barbarossa.* New York: William Morrow and Co., 1965.

Clausewitz, Carl von. *On War.* Michael Howard and Peter Paret eds. and trans. Princeton: Princeton University Press, 1976.

Cole, Hugh M. *The Ardennes: Battle of the Bulge.* Washington: Department of the Army, 1965.

Cooling, Benjamin Franklin, ed. *Case Studies in the Development of Close Air Support.* Washington: Office of Air Force History, 1990.

Cooper, Matthew. *The German Army, 1933–1945*. New York: Stein and Day, 1979.

———. *The Nazi War Against Soviet Partisans, 1941–1944*. New York: Stein and Day, 1979.

Corum, James S. *The Roots of Blitzkrieg*. Lawrence: University Press of Kansas, 1992.

———. "The Luftwaffe's Army Support Doctrine, 1918–1941." *The Journal of Military History*. Vol. 59, No. 1, (January 1995): pp. 53–76.

Craig, Gordon. *The Politics of the Prussian Army, 1660–1945*. New York: Oxford University Press, 1955.

———. *Germany, 1866–1945*. New York: Oxford University Press, 1978.

Craig, William. *Enemy at the Gates*. New York: E. P. Dutton and Company, Inc., 1973.

Creveld, Martin van. *Supplying War*. London: Cambridge University Press, 1977.

———. *Fighting Power*. Westport: Greenwood Press, 1982.

Crow, Duncan, ed. *Armored Fighting Vehicles of Germany*. New York: Arco Publishing Company, Inc. 1978.

Dallin, Alexander. *German Rule in Russia, 1941-1945*. 2nd ed. Boulder: Westview Press, 1981.

Daugherty, Leo J. III. "The Volksdeutsche and Hitler's War." *The Journal of Slavic Military Studies*. Vol. 8, No. 2, (June 1995): pp. 296–318.

Davies, W.J.K. *German Army Handbook, 1939—945*. New York: Arco Publishing Company, Inc., 1974.

DeBeaulieu, Walter Charles. *Der Vorstoss der Panzergruppe 4 auf Leningrad*. Neckargemund: Kurt Vowinckel Verlag, 1961.

De Gaulle, General Charles. *The Army of the Future*. Philadelphia: J. B. Lippincott, 1941.

Deist, Wilhelm. *The Wehrmacht and German Rearmament*. London: The Macmillan Press Ltd., 1981.

———, ed. *The German Military in the Age of Total War*. Dover: Berg Publishers Limited, 1985.

Department of the Army. Pamphlet #20-201, Military Improvisations During the Russian Campaign. Washington, D.C.: Department of the Army, 1951.

————. Pamphlet #20-234, Operations of Encircled Forces. Washington, D.C.: Department of the Army, 1952.

D'Este, Carlo. *Decision in Normandy*. New York: E. P. Dutton, Inc., 1983.

————. *Bitter Victory*. E. P. Dutton, Inc. 1988.

Detwiler, Donald, ed. *World War II German Military Studies*. 14 Vols. New York: Garland Publishing, Inc., 1979.

Dickens, Peter. *Night Action*. New York: Bantam Books, 1981.

DiNardo, R. L. *Mechanized Juggernaut or Military Anachronism?: Horses and the German Army of World War II*. Westport: Greenwood Press, 1991.

————. "The Dysfunctional Coalition: The Axis Powers and the Eastern Front in World War II." *The Journal of Military History*. Vol. 60, No. 4, (October 1996): pp. 711–730.

————. "The Armored Fist." *Strategy and Tactics*. Special Issue #4. (October 1984): pp. 14–32.

————. "German Armor Doctrine: Correcting the Myths." *War in History*. Vol. 3, No. 4, (November 1996): pp. 384–397.

DiNardo, R. L., and Bay, Austin. "Horse-Drawn Transport in the German Army." *Journal of Contemporary History*. Vol. 23, No. 1, (January 1988): pp. 129–142.

Doubler, Michael D. *Closing with the Enemy*. Lawrence: University Press of Kansas, 1994.

Doughty, Robert Allan. *The Seeds of Disaster*. Hamden: Archon Books, 1985.

————. *The Breaking Point*. Hamden: Archon Books, 1990.

Duffy, Christopher. *The Army of Frederick the Great*. New York: Hippocrene Books, 1974.

Dupuy, Trevor N. *A Genius For War*. Englewood: Prentice-Hall Inc., 1977.

————, and Martel, Paul. *Great Battles on the Eastern Front*. New York: The Bobbs Merrill Company, Inc., 1982.

Echevarria, Antulio II. "Moltke and the German Military Tradition: His Theories and Legacy." *Parameters*. Vol. XXVI, No. 1, (Spring 1996): pp. 91–99.

Eimannsberger, General Ludwig Ritter von. *Der Kampfwagenkrieg*. Berlin, J. F., Lehmanns Verlag, 1938.

————. "Panzertaktik." *Militär Wochenblatt*. Vol. 121, No. 26, (8 January 1937): pp. 1447–1453.

————. "Panzertaktik II." *Militär Wochenblatt.* Vol. 121, No. 27, (15 January 1937): pp. 1509–1516.

Eisenhower, General Dwight D. *Crusade in Europe.* New York: Garden City Books, 1951.

Ellis, L. F. *The War in France and Flanders, 1939–1940.* London: Her Majesty's Stationary Office, 1953.

Engelmann, Joachim. *Zitadelle.* Dorheim: Podzun-Pallas-Verlag GmbH., 1982.

Engster, Captain. "Kampfwagen und Nebel." *Militär Wochenblatt.* Vol. 115, No 42, (11 May 1931): pp. 1633–1638.

English, John A. *On Infantry.* New York: Praeger Publishers, 1981.

Erickson, John. *The Soviet High Command.* London: St. Martin's press, 1962.

————. *The Road to Stalingrad.* New York: Harper and Row, Publishers, 1975.

————. *The Road to Berlin.* Boulder: Westview Press, 1983. "Eurollydon," "The Psychology of the German Regimental Officer." *Royal United Service Institution Journal.* Vol. LXXXII, No. 528, (November 1937): pp, 772–777.

Fenyo, Mario D. *Hitler, Horthy and Hungary.* New Haven: Yale University Press 1972.

Fest, Joachim C. *Hitler.* New York: Vintage Books, 1975.

Fleischer, Wolfgang. "Die Feldartillerie des Heeres in der Panzerabwehr 1939–1945." *Militär Geschichte.* Vol. 1, No. 1, (Winter 1994): pp. 9–15.

Frankel, Nat, and Smith, Larry. *Patton's Best.* New York: Hawthorn Books, Inc., 1978.

Fritz, Stephen G. *Frontsoldaten.* Lexington: The University Press of Kentucky, 1995.

Fuchtbauer, Colonel Heinrich Ritter von. "Der Vernichtungsgedanke—entscheidend auch in der neuzeitlich Kriegführung!" *Militär Wochenblatt* Vol. 117, No. 32, (11 September 1932): pp. 318–320.

Fugate, Bryan I. *Operation Barbarossa.* Novato: Presidio Press, 1984.

Fuller, Major General J.F.C. *On Future Warfare.* London: Sifton Praed and Co., Ltd., 1928.

————. *Lectures on FSR III.* London: Eyre and Spotiswood, Ltd., 1928.

————. *Memoirs of an Unconventinal Soldier.* London: Ivor Nicholson and Watson, Ltd., 1936.

————. *Armored Warfare.* Harrisburg: Military Services Publishing Company, 1943.

Gallwitz, First Lieutenant Uto. "Beiträge zur Kampfwagenabwehr." *Militär Wochenblatt.* Vol. 111, No. 9, (4 September 1926): pp. 294–299.

————. "Infanteriegeschütz and Kampfwagenabwehr." *Militär Wochenblatt.* Vol. 111, No. 14, (11 October 1926): pp. 485–487.

Gatzke, Hans W. "Russo-German Military Collaboration During the Weimat Republic." *American Historical Review.* Vol. LXIII, No. 3, (April 1958): pp. 565–597.

Glantz, David M., and House, Jonathan. *When Titans Clashed: How the Red Army Stopped Hitler.* Lawrence: University Press of Kansas, 1995.

Gooch, John. *Armies in Europe.* London: Routledge and Kegan Paul Ltd., 1980.

Goralski, Robert, and Freeburg, Russell W. *Oil and War.* New York: William Morrow and Company, Inc., 1987.

Görlitz, Walter. *History of the German General Staff.* New York: Praeger Publishers, 1953.

————. *Paulus and Stalingrad.* New York: The Citadel Press, 1963.

Gravenhorst, First Lieutenant R. "Verwendung der Luftwaffe im Erdkampf." *Militär Wochenblatt.* Vol. 120, No. 33, (4 March 1936): pp. 1459–1460.

Greenfield, Kent Roberts, et al. *The Organization of Ground Combat Troops.* Washington: Department of the Army, 1947.

Griffith, Paddy. *Forward into Battle.* New York: Hippocrene Books, Inc., 1981.

Grunberger. Richard. *A Social History of the Third Reich.* London: Weidenfeld and Nicolson, 1971.

Grundel, Gunther. "Die Krise des Vernichtungsgedankens in der neuzeitlichen Kriegführung." *Militär Wochenblatt.* Vol. 117, No. 7, (18 August 1932): pp. 209–212.

Guderian, General Heinz. *Panzer Leader.* New York: E. P. Dutton, Inc., 1952.

————. *Errinerungen eines Soldaten.* Heidelberg: Kurt Vowinckel Verlag, 1951.

————. *Achtung-Panzer!* Stuttgart: Union Deutsche Verlagsgesellschaft, 1937.

————. "Truppen auf Kraftwagen und Fliegerabwehr." *Militär Wochenblatt.* Vol. 109, No. 12, (25 September 1924): pp. 305–306.

————. "Heeresekavallerie und motorisierte Verbände." *Militär Wochenblatt.* Vol. 119, No. 34, (11 March 1935): pp. 1338–1339.

————. "Kraftfahrtruppen." *Militärwissenschaftliche Rundschau.* Vol. 1, No. 1, (December 1935): pp. 52–78.

————. "Die Panzertruppen und ihr Zusammenwirken mit den anderen Waffen." *Militärwissenschaftliche Rundschau.* Vol. 1, No. 5 (March 1936): pp. 607–626.

————. "Schnell Truppen einst und jetzt." *Militärwissenschaftliche Rundschau.* Vol. 4, No. 2, (March 1939): pp. 229–243.

Gunsberg, Jeffry A. "The Battle of the Belgian Plain, 12–14 May: The First Great Tank Battle." *The Journal of Military History.* Vol. 56, No. 2, (April 1992): pp. 207–244.

Halder, General Franz. *The Halder Diaries.* 7 Vols. Washington, D.C.: U.S. Army, 1950.

Hancock, Eleanor. "Ernst Röhm and the Experience of World War I" *The Journal of Military History.* Vol. 60, No. 1, (January 1996): pp. 39–60.

Harrison, Gordon A. *Cross-Channel Attack.* Washington, D.C.: Department of the Army, 1951.

Hartness, Captain Harland. "Germany's Tactical Doctrine." *Infantry Journal.* Vol. XLVI, No. 3, (June 1939): pp. 249–251.

Hastings, Max. *Das Riech.* New York: Holt, Rinehart and Winston, 1981.

Haupt, Werner. *Heeresgruppe Nord.* Bad Neuheim: Podzun Verlag, 1966.

————. *Heeresgruppe Mitte.* Dorheim: Podzun Verlag, 1968.

————. *Die Schlachten der Heeresgruppe Süd.* Bad Neuheim: Podzun Verlag, 1985.

Hausser, Paul. *Soldaten Wie Andere Auch.* Osnabrück: Munin Verlag GmbH., 1966.

Hayes, Peter. *Industry and Ideology.* New York: Cambridge University Press, 1987.

Heckmann, Wolf. *Rommel's War in Africa.* New York: Doubleday and Company, Inc., 1981.

Heigl, Fritz. *Taschenbuch der Tanks*. München: J. F. Lehmanns Verlag, 1927.

Herzstein, Robert Edwin. *The War that Hitler Won*. New York: Paragon House Publishers, 1987.

Higgins, Major George A. "German and U.S. Operational Art: A Contrast in Maneuver." *Military Review*. Vol. LXV., No. 10, (October 1985): pp. 22–29.

Higgins, Trumbull. *Hitler and Russia*. New York: The Macmillan Company, 1966.

Higham, Robin. *The Military Intellectuals in Britain: 1918–1939*. New Brunswick: Rutgers University Press, 1966.

Hinze, Rolf. *Der Zusammenbruch der Heeresgruppe Mitte im Osten, 1944*. Stuttgart: Motorbuch Verlag, 1980.

Hitler, Adolf. *Hitler's Secret Book*. New York: Grove Press, Inc., 1961.

———. *Hitler's Secret Conversations, 1941–1944*. New York: Farrar, Strauss and Young, 1953.

———. *Mein Kampf*. Reprinted ed. Boston: The Houghton Mifflin Company, 1971.

Höhne, Heinz. *The Order of the Death's Head*. New York: Ballantine Books, 1971.

Hossbach, General Friedrich. *Zwischen Wehrmacht und Hitler*. Hannover: Wolfenbutteler Verlagsanstalt GmbH., 1949.

Hoth, General Hermann. *Panzer-Operationen*. Heidelberg: Kurt Vowinckel Verlag, 1956.

House, Captain Jonathan M. *Towards Combined Arms Warfare*. Fort Leavenworth: U.S. Army, 1984.

Houston, Donald E. *Hell on Wheels*. San Rafael: Presidio Press, 1977.

Howard, Michael, ed. *The Theory and Practice of War*. Bloomington: Indiana University Press, 1965.

Hughes, Daniel J., ed. *Molike on the Art of War: Selected Writings*. Novato: Presidio Press., 1993.

———. "Abuses of German Military History." *Military Review*. Vol. LXVI, No. 12, (December 1986): pp. 66–76.

———. "Schlichting, Schlieffen, and the Prussian Theory of War in 1914." *The Journal of Military History*. Vol. 59, No. 2, (April 1995): pp. 257–277.

Icks, Robert J. *Famous Tank Battles*. New York: Doubleday and Co., Inc., 1972.

Irving, David. *The Trail of the Fox*. New York: Avon Books, 1978.

————. *The War Path.* New York: The Viking Press, 1978.

Jacobsen, Hans-Adolf. *Fall Gelb.* Wiesbaden: Franz Steiner Verlag GmbH., 1957.

————, and Rohwer, Jürgen, eds. *Decisive Battles of World War II: The German View.* New York: G. P. Putnam's Sons, 1965.

Jukes, Geoffrey. *Hitler's Stalingrad Decisions.* Berkeley: University of California Press, 1985.

Keegan, John. *Six Armies in Normandy.* New York: The Viking Press, 1982.

Kehrig, Manfred. *Stalingrad.* Stuttgart: Deutsche-Verlags Anstalt, 1974.

Keilig, Wolf. *Das Deutsche Heer, 1939–1945.* 3 Vols. Bad Neuheim: Podzun Verlag, 1963.

Keitel, Field Marshal Wilhelm. *In the Service of the Reich.* New York: Stein and Day, 1966.

Kennedy, Robert M. *The German Campaign in Poland (1939).* Washington, D.C.: U.S. Army, 1956.

Kesselring, Field Marshal Albert. *Kesselring: A Soldier's Record.* New York: William Morrow, 1953.

Klein, Burton H. *Germany's Economic Preparations For War.* Cambridge: Harvard University Press, 1959.

Kleinfeld, Gerald R. "Hitler's Strike For Tikhvin." *Military Affairs.* Vol. XLVII, No. 3, (October 1983): pp. 122–128.

Klink, Ernst. *Das Gesetz des Handelns: Die Operation "Zitadelle."* Stuttgart: Deutsche-Verlags Anstalt GmbH., 1966.

Knoerzer, General Hans. "Hannibal und Hindenburg, ein zeitgemasser Vergleich." *Militär Wochenblatt.* Vol. 106, No. 13, (24 September 1921): pp. 265–268.

Koch, H. W. *The Hitler Youth.* New York: Stein and Day, 1976.

Koehl, Robert Lewis. *The Black Corps.* Madison: University of Wisconsin Press, 1983.

Kurowski, Franz. *Die Panzer-Lehr Division.* Bad Neuheim: Podzun Verlag, 1964.

Larson, Robert H. *The British Army and the Theory of Armored Warfare, 1918–1940.* Newark: University of Delaware Press, 1984.

Leeb, Field Marshal Wilhelm Ritter von. *Die Abwehr.* Berlin: E. S. Mittler und Sohn, 1938.

Lehmann, Rudolf. *Die Leibstandarte.* 3 Vols. Osnabrück: Munin Verlag GmbH., 1977–1982.

Lewin, Ronald. *Hitler's Mistakes.* New York: William Morrow, 1984.

Lewis, S. J. *Forgotten Legions.* New York: Praeger Publishers, 1985.

Liddell-Hart, Basil H. *Paris or the Future of War.* New York: E. P. Dutton, 1925.

———. *The Remaking of Modern Armies.* London: John Murray, 1927.

———. *The Future of Infantry.* London: Faber and Faber, Ltd., 1933.

———. *The German Generals Talk.* New York: William Morrow, 1948.

———, ed. *The Rommel Papers.* New York: Harcourt Brace, 1953.

———. *The Tanks.* 2 Vols. New York: Frederick A. Praeger Publishers, 1959.

———. *Strategy.* New York: Praeger Publishers, 1967.

———. *History of the Second World War.* New York: Capricorn Books, 1972.

Lochner, Louis P., ed. *The Goebbels Diaries, 1942–1943.* New York: Doubleday, 1948.

Lucas, James. *War on the Eastern Front, 1941–1945.* New York: Bonanza Books, 1979.

Luck, Colonel Hans von. *Panzer Commander.* New York: Praeger Publishers, 1989.

Ludendorff, General Erich. *Tannenberg: Geschichtliche Wahrheit über die Schlacht.* München: Ludendorffs Verlag, 1939.

Lukacs, John. *The Last European War.* New York: Anchor Press, 1976.

Lupfer, Captain Timothy T. *The Dynamics of Doctrine: The Changes in German Tactical Doctrine During the First World War.* Fort Leavenworth: Combat Studies Institute, 1981.

Luvaas, Jay. *A Time For Trumpets.* New York: William Morrow, 1985.

Mackensen, General Eberhard von. *Vom Bug zum Kaukasus.* Neckargemund: Scharnhorst Buchkameradschaft, 1967.

Macksey, Kenneth. *Guderian: Panzer General.* London: Macdonald and Jane's, 1975.

———. *Tank Warfare.* New York: Stein and Day, 1972.

Manstein, Field Marshal Erich von. *Lost Victories.* Reprinted Ed. Novato: Presidio Press, 1982.

———. *Aus Einem Soldatenleben, 1887–1939.* Bonn: Athenäun Verlag, 1958.

Manteuffel, General Baron Hasso von. *Die 7. Panzer Division im Zweiten Weltkrieg.* Ürdingen-am-Rhein: Traditionsverband Ehem 7. Panzer Division Kameradhilfe, 1965.

Mastny, Vojtech. *The Czechs Under Nazi Rule.* New York: Columbia University Press, 1971.

Mearsheimer, John J. *Liddell-Hart and the Weight of History.* Ithaca: Cornell University Press, 1988.

Mellenthin, Major General Friedrich Wilhelm von. *Panzer Battles.* New York: Ballantine Books, 1971.

———. *German Generals of World War II.* Norman: University of Oklahoma Press, 1977.

Messenger, Charles. *Hitler's Gladiator.* New York: Brassey's Defense Publishers, 1988.

———. *The Last Prussian.* London: Brassey's, 1991.

Miksche, Major F. O. *Blitzkrieg.* London: Faber and Faber, 1941. Militärgeschichtlichen Forschungsamt. *Das Deutsche Reich und der Zweite Weltkrieg.* 6 Vols. Stuttgart: Deutsche Verlags-Anstalt, 1979–1991.

Millett, Allan R., and Murray, Williamson, eds. *Military Effectiveness.* 3 Vols. Boston: Allen and Unwin, 1988.

Milward, Alan S. *The German Economy at War.* London: The Athlone Press, 1965.

Mitchell, Brian R. *European Historical Statistics, 1750–1975.* 2nd Rev. Ed. New York: Facts on File, 1981.

Moltke, Field Marshal Helmut, Graf von. *Ausgewählte Werke.* F. von Schmerfeld ed. 4 Vols. Berlin: Verlag von Reimar Hobbing, 1925.

Morelock, Major Jerry D. "The Legacy of Liddell-Hart." *Military Review.* Vol. LXVI, No. 5, (May 1986): pp. 65–75.

Mueller, Gordon H. "Rapallo Reexamined: A New Look at Germany's Secret Military Collaboration With Russia in 1922." *Military Affairs.* Vol. 40, No. 3, (October 1976): pp. 109–116.

Müller, Klaus-Jürgen. *Armee, Politik and Gesellschaft in Deutschland, 1933–1945.* Paderborn: Ferdinand Schöningh, 1979.

———. *General Ludwig Beck.* Boppard-am-Rhein: Harald Boldt Verlag, 1980.

Müller, Major General Kurt. "Mechanisierung und Motorisierung." *Militär Wochenblatt.* Vol. 117, No. 25, (4 January 1933): p. 833.

Müller, Richard. *The German Air War in Russia.* Baltimore: Nautical and Aviation Publishing Company, 1992.

Müller-Hillebrand, Burkhart. *Das Heer, 1933–45.* 3 Vols. Frankfurt-am-Main: E. S. Mittler und Sohn, 1954–1969.

————. *German Tank Maintenance in World War II*. Washington, D.C.: Department of the Army, 1954.

Munzel, Oscar. *Panzer-Taktik*. Neckargemund: Kurt Vowinckel Verlag, 1959.

Murray, Williamson. *The Change in the European Balance of Power, 1938–1939*. Princeton: Princeton University Press, 1984.

————. *Luftwaffe*. Baltimore: The Nautical and Aviation Publishing Company of America, Inc., 1985.

————. "The German Response to Victory in Poland: A Case Study in Professionalism." *Armed Forces and Society*. Vol. 7, No. 2, (Winter 1981): pp. 285–298.

Nehring, General Walter. *Die Geschichte der Deutschen Panzerwaffe, 1916 bis 1945*. Berlin: Propyläen Verlag, 1969.

————. *Panzerabwehr*. Berlin: E. S. Mittler und Sohn, 1936.

————. "Panzerabwehr." *Militärwissenschaftliche Rundschau*. Vol. 1, No. 2, (March 1936): pp. 182–203.

Neumann, Peter. *The Black March*. New York: Bantam Books, 1960.

Niepold, Gerd. *Battle For White Russia*. New York: Brassey's Defense Publishers, 1987.

Nofi, Albert, ed. *The War Against Hitler*. New York: Hippocrene Books, 1982.

Nove, Alec. *An Economic History of the USSR*. New York: Penguin Books, 1969.

Ogorkiewicz, Richard. *Armor*. New York: Frederick A. Praeger Publishers, 1960.

Orgill, Douglas. *The Tank*. London: William Heineman, 1970.

Ose, Dieter. *Entscheidung im Westen, 1944*. Stuttgart: Deutsche Verlags-Anstalt, 1982.

————. "Rommel and Rundstedt: The 1944 Panzer Controversy." *Military Affairs*. Vol. 50, No. 1, (January): pp. 7–11.

Overy, Richard J. *Göring: The "Iron Man."* London: Routledge and Kegan Paul, 1984.

————. *War and Economy in the Third Reich*. London: Oxford University Press, 1994.

————. *Why the Allies Won*. New York: W. W. Norton and Company, 1995.

Padfield, Peter. *Himmler*. New York: Henry Holt and Company, 1990.

Paret, Peter, ed. *The Makers of Modern Strategy*. Princeton: Princeton University Press, 1986.

Paul, Wolfgang. *Panzer-General Walter K. Nehring.* Stuttgart: Motorbuch Verlag, 1986.

Pearton, Maurice. *Oil and the Romanian State.* New York: Oxford University Press, 1971.

Perkins, John. "Coins For Conflict: Nickel and the Axis, 1933–1945." *The Historian.* Vol. 55, No. 1, (Autumn 1992): pp. 85–100.

Perrett, Bryan. *A History of Blitzkrieg.* New York: Stein and Day, 1983.

———. *Knights of the Black Cross.* New York: St. Martin's Press, 1986.

Philippi, Alfred, and Heim, Ferdinand. *Der Feldzug gegen Sowjetrussland.* Stuttgart: W. Kohlhammer Verlag, 1962.

Pitt, Barrie. *The Crucible of War.* London: Jonathan Cape, 1980.

Poseck, General Max von. "Die Kavalllerie im Manover 1930." *Militär Wochenblatt.* Vol. 115, No. 21, (4 December 1930): pp. 793–797.

———. "Kavallerie von einst und jetzt." *Militär Wochenblatt.* Vol. 118, No. 43 (18 May 1934): pp. 1464–1468.

———. "Aus grosser Zeit vor zwanzig Jahren. Kriegserfahrungen in der Verwen dung moderner Kavallerie." *Militär Wochenblatt.* Vol. 119, No. 30, (1 February 1935): pp. 1171–1175.

———. "Aus grosser Zeit vor zwanzig Jahren. Kriegserfahrungen in der Verwen dung moderner Kavallerie." *Militär Wochenblatt.* Vol. 119, No. 31, (1 Febraury 1935): pp. 1211–1213.

Posen, Barry R. *The Sources of Military Doctrine.* Ithaca: Cornell University Press, 1984.

Prüller, Wilhelm. *Diary of a German Soldier.* H. C. Robbins Landon and Sebastian Leitner eds. London: Faber and Faber, 1963.

Rauschning, Hermann. *Hitler Speaks.* London: T. Butterworth, 1939.

Reinhardt, Klaus. *Die Wende vor Moskau.* Stuttgart: Deutsche Verlags-Anstal 1972.

Reinicke, General Georg. "Kampfwagenabwehr." *Militär Wochenblatt.* Vol. 120, No. 39, (20 April 1936): pp. 1753–1754.

Rempel, Gerhard. *Hitler's Children.* Chapel Hill: University of North Carolir Press, 1989.

Rich, Norman. *Hitler's War Arms.* New York: W. W. Norton, 1973.

Richardson, Horst Fuchs, and Showalter, Dennis E., eds. *Sieg Heil!: War Letters of Tank Gunner Karl Fuchs, 1937–1941.* Hamden: Archon Books, 1987.

Ritgen, Helmut. *Die Geschichte der Panzer Lehr Division im Westen, 1944–1945.* Stuttgart: Motorbuch Verlag, 1979.

Rogers, H.C.B. *Tanks in Battle*. London: Seeley Service, 1965.

Rohde, Horst. *Das Deutsche Wehrmachttransportwesen im Zweiten Weltkrie*. Stuttgart: Deutsche Verlags-Anstalt, 1971.

Rommel, Field Marshal Erwin. *Infantry Attacks*. Vienna, Va.: Athena Press, 1979.

Ross, General George MacLeod. *The Business of Tanks, 1933 to 1945*. Devon: Arthur H. Stockwell, 1976.

Rothbrust, Florian K. *Guderian's XIXth Panzer Corps and the Battle of France*. New York: Praeger Publishers, 1990.

Rotundo, Louis, ed. *The Battle For Stalingrad*. New York: Pergamon-Brassey's, 1989.

Sajer, Guy. *The Forgotten Soldier*. New York: Ballantine Books, 1972.

Scheibert, Horst. *Einsatzversuch Stalingrad*. Neckargemund: Kurt Vowinckel Verlag, 1968.

Schramm, Percy Ernst. *Hitler: The Man and the Military Leader*. Chicago: Quadrangle Books, 1971.

Schülze-Kossens, Richard. *Militärischer Führernachwuchs der Waffen-SS: die Junkerschulen*. Osnabrück: Munin Verlag, 1982.

Seaton, Albert. *The German Army, 1933–45*. New York: St. Martin's Press, 1982.

———. *The Fall of Fortress Europe, 1943–1945*. New York: Holmes and Meier Publications, 1981.

———. *Stalin as Military Commander*. New York: Praeger Publishers, 1976.

———. *The Russo-German War, 1941–45*. New York: Praeger Publishers, 1970.

Seeckt, General Hans von. *Thoughts of a Soldier*. London: Faber and Faber, 1930.

Sella, Amnon. "Barbarossa: Surprise Attack and Communications." *Journal of Contemporary History*. Vol. 13, No. 3, (July 1978): pp. 555–585.

Senff, Hubertus. *Die Entwicklung der Panzerwaffe im deutschen Heer zwischen den beiden Weltkriegen*. Frankfurt-am-Main: E. S. Mittler und Sohn, 1969.

Senger und Etterlin, General F. M. von. *Die Deutschen Panzer, 1926–1945*. München: J. F. Lehmanns Verlag, 1965.

———. *Neither Fear Nor Hope*. New York: E. P. Dutton,. 1964.

———. *Die Panzergrenadiere*. München: J. F. Lehmanns Verlag, 1961.

Senger und Etterlin, Fridolin von, Jr. *Die 24. Panzer Division vormals 1. Kavallerie-Division, 1939–1945.* Neckargemund: Kurt Vowinckel Verlag, 1962.

Sheppard, G. A. *The Italian Campaign, 1943–45.* London: Arthur Barker, 1968.

Showalter, Dennis E. *Tannenberg: Clash of Empires.* Hamden: Archon Books, 1991.

Shulman, Milton. *Defeat in the West.* New York: E. P. Dutton, 1948.

Simpkin, Richard. *Deep Battle.* New York: Brassey's Defense Publishers, 1987.

Sorge, Martin K. *The Other Price of Hitler's War.* Westport: Greenwood Press, 1986.

Souter, Kevin. "To Stem the Red Tide: The German Report Series and Its Effect on American Defense Doctrine, 1948–1954." *The Journal of Military History.* Vol. 57, No. 4, (October 1993): pp. 653–688.

Spannenkrebs, Lieutenant Colonel Walter. *Angriff mit Kampfwagen.* Berlin: Gerhard Stalling Verlagsbuchhandlung, 1939.

Speer, Albert. *Inside the Third Reich.* New York: Macmillan, 1970.

Speidel, Lieutenant General Hans. *Invasion 1944.* Reprinted ed. Westport: Greenwood Press, 1971.

Spielberger, Walter J. *Panzer III & Its Variants.* Atglen, Pa.: Schiffer Publishing, 1993.

———. *Panther & Its Variants.* Atglen, Pa.: Schiffer Publishing, 1993.

———. *Panzer IV & Its Variants.* Atglen, Pa.: Schiffer Publishing, 1993.

Spires, David N. *Image and Reality.* Westport: Greenwood Press, 1984.

Stadler, Sylvester. *Die Offensive gegen Kursk, 1943.* Osnabrück: Munin Verlag, 1980.

Steiger, Rudolf. *Panzertaktik im Spiegel deutscher Kriegstagebucher, 1939–1941.* Freiburg-im-Breisgau: Verlag Rombach Freiburg, 1973.

Stein, George H. *The Waffen SS.* Ithaca: Cornell University Press, 1966.

Steinert, Marlis G. *Hitler's War and the Germans.* Athens: Ohio University Press, 1977.

Stewart, Richard W. "The 'Red Bull' Division: The Training and Initial Engagements of the 34th Infantry Division." *Army History.* No. 25, (Winter 1993): pp. 1–10.

Stolfi, R.H.S. "Barbarossa Revisited: A Critical Reappraisal of the Opening Stages of the Russo-German Campaign." *The Journal of Modern History*. Vol. 54, No. 1, (March 1992): pp. 27–46.

Stone, Norman. *The Eastern Front, 1914-1917*. New York: Charles Scribner's Sons, 1975.

Stoves, Rolf. *Die 22. Panzer-Division, 25. Panzer-Division, 27. Panzer-Division and die 233. Reserve-Panzer-Division*. Bad Neuheim: Podzun-PallasVerlag, 1985.

————. *Die 1. Panzer Division*. Bad Neuheim: Podzun Verlag, 1961.

Strassner, Peter. *Europäische Freiwillige*. Osnabrück: Munin Verlag, 1968.

Sweet, John J. T. *Mounting the Threat*. San Rafael: Presidio Press, 1977.

Sydnor, Charles. *Soldiers of Destruction*. Princeton: Princeton University Press, 1977.

Taylor, Telford. *The March of Conquest*. New York: Simon and Schuster, 1958.

Terraine, John. *The Right of the Line*. London: Hodder and Stoughton, 1985.

Tessin, Georg. *Verbände und Truppen der deutschen Wehrmacht und Waffen SS im Zweiten Weltkrieg, 1939–1945*. 14 Vols. Osnabrück: Biblio Verlag, 1977.

Thomas, General Georg. *Geschichte der deutschen Wehr und Rüstungswirtschaft*. Boppard-am-Rhein: Harald Boldt Verlag, 1966.

Tiberi, Lieutenant Colonel Paul. "German versus Soviet Blitzkrieg." *Military Review*. Vol. LXV, No. 9, (September 1985): pp. 63–71.

Tieke, Wilhelm. *Der Kaukasus und das Öl*. Osnabrück: Munin Verlag, 1970.

Tippelskirch, General Kurt von. *Geschichte des Zweiten Weltkriegs*. Bonn: Athenäum-Verlag, 1951.

Traditionsverband der Ehem 3. Panzer Division. *Geschichte der 3. Panzer-Division*. Berlin: Verlag der Buchhandlung Gunther Richer, 1967.

Trevor-Roper, Hugh R. *Hitler's War Directives, 1939–1945*. London: Sidgwick and Jackson, 1964.

Trythall, Anthony John. *"Boney" Fuller*. New Brunswick: Rutgers University Press, 1977.

United States Strategic Bombing Survey. "Summary Report." 30 September 1945. Washington, D.C.: Government Printing Office.

————. "Overall Report." 30 September 1945. Washington, D.C.: Government Printing Office.

————. "The Effects of Strategic Bombing on the German War Economy." 31 October 1945. Washington, D.C.: Government Printing Office.

————. "German Motor Vehicle Industry Report." January 1947. Washington, D.C.: Government Printing Office.

————. "Tank Industry Report." 2nd Ed. January 1947. Washington, D.C.: Government Printing Office.

————. "Statistical Appendix to Overall Report." February 1947. Washington, D.C.: Government Printing Office.

Unsigned. "Die Französischen Tanks im Weltkrieg." *Militär Wochenblatt.* Vol. 105, No. 32, (5 February 1921): pp. 700–702.

————. "Funkverbindung zwischen Kampfwagen." *Militär Wochenblatt.* Vol. 111, No. 40, (25 April 1927): pp. 1485–1486.

————. "Gedanken uber das Zusammenwirken der Pionere mit den anderen Waffen." *Militär Wochenblatt.* Vol. 121, No. 4, (25 July 1936): pp. 170–174.

————. "Gedanken uber das Zusammenwirken der Pionere mit den anderen Waffen." *Militär Wochenblatt.* Vol. 121, No. 5, (4 August 1936): pp. 222–226.

————. "Gedanken uber das Zusammenwirken der Pionere mit den anderen Waffen." *Militär Wochenblatt.* Vol. 121, No. 6, (11 August 1936): pp. 281–284.

————. "Gliederung neuzeitlicher Truppenkorper." *Militär Wochenblatt.* Vol. 119, No. 12, (18 September 1934): pp. 407–410.

————. "Gliederung neuzeitlicher Truppenkorper." *Militär Wochenblatt.* Vol. 119, No. 13, (25 September 1934): pp. 448–450.

————. "Der Infanterie-Angriff in französischen Heere." *Militärwissenschaftliche Rundschau.* Vol. 4, No. 3, (May 1939): pp. 422–442.

————. "Infanterie and Kampfwagen auf Grund der französischen Kampfwagenverwendung." *Militär Wochenblatt.* Vol. 113, No. 5, (4 August 1928): pp. 175–177.

————. "International Military Survey." *Infantry Journal.* Vol. XLVI, No. 6, (December 1939): pp. 591–597.

————. "Die Kampfwagen der Gegenwart." *Militär Wochenblatt.* Vol. 116, No. 12, (25 September 1931): pp. 433–439.

————. "Die Kampfwagen der Gegenwart." *Militär Wochenblatt.* Vol. 116, No. 13, (4 October 1931): pp. 469–474.

————. "Kampfwagen und Kavallerie." *Militär Wochenblatt.* Vol. 111, No. 38, (11 April 1927): pp. 1405–1406.

————. "Kampfwagenausbildung in Russland." *Militär Wochenblatt.* Vol. 111, No. 13, (4 October 1926): pp. 444–445.

————. "Kavallerie—oder Motorisierungsproblem?" *Militär Wochenblatt.* Vol. 119, No. 11, (4 August 1934): pp. 164–167.

————. "Militärpolitisches über England." *Militär Wochenblatt.* Vol. 110, No. 12, (25 September 1925): pp. 405–407.

————. "Panzerjäger!" *Wochenblatt.* Vol. 121, No. 13, (4 October 1936): pp. 636–638.

————. "Panzerjäger oder Panzerkampfwagen." *Militär Wochenblatt.* Vol. 121, No. 11, (18 September 1936): pp. 535–537.

————. "Die Panazerwaffe in Fernost." *Militär Wochenblatt.* Vol. 117, No. 13, (4 October 1932): pp. 417–423.

————. "Das Pferd in Heer and Wirtschaft von heute." *Militär Wochenblatt.* Vol. 121, No. 41, (23 April 1937): pp. 2537–2540.

————. "Pionere and Panzerabwehr." *Militär Wochenblatt.* Vol. 120, No. 31, (18 February 1936): pp. 1382–1384.

————. "Die Rangabzeichen der SA." *Militär Wochenblatt.* Vol. 118, No. 11, (18 September 1933): p. 363.

————. "Revolution des Krieges." *Militär Wochenblatt.* Vol. 117, No. 19, (18 November 1932): pp. 617–623.

————. "Tank gegen Tank." *Militär Wochenblatt.* Vol. 120, No. 25, (4 January 1936): pp. 1084–1086.

————. "Tankbekampfung durch Minen." *Militar Wochenblatt.* Vol. 118, No. 8, (25 August 1933): pp. 250–251.

————. "Zusammenarbeit von Kampfwagen und Artillerie beim Angriff." *Militär Wochenblatt.* Vol. 115, No. 48, (25 June 1931): pp. 1885–1886.

————. "Zusammenwirken von Panzerkampfwagen mit Kavallerie. " *Militär Wochenblatt,* Vol. 115, No. 33, (4 March 1931): pp. 1282–1284.

Volckheim, Ernst. *Die deutschen Kampfwagen im Weltkriege.* Berlin: E. S. Mittler und Sohn, 1923.

————. *Der Kampfwagen in der heutigen Kriegführung.* Berlin: E. S. Mittler und Sohn, 1924.

————. "Die Kampfwagenfrage." *Militär Wochenblatt.* Vol. 108, No. 20,(25 June 1924): pp. 718–721.

Wagener, Carl. *Heeresgruppe Süd.* Bad Neuheim: Podzun Verlag, 1967.

Wagenführ, Rolf. *Die Deutsche Industrie im Kriege, 1939–1945.* Berlin: Deutsches Institut für Wirtschaftsforschung, 1955.

Wagner, Major Hans. "Gedanken uber Kampfwagenabwehr." *Militär Wochenblatt.* Vol. 113, No. 4, (4 July 1928): pp. 10–12.

———. "Tankkarten und Tankforts." *Militär Wochenblatt.* Vol. 113, No. 10, (11 September 1928): pp. 377–380.

Walde, Karl J. *Guderian.* Berlin: Verlag Ullstein, 1976.

Wallach, Jehuda L. *The Dogma of the Battle of Annihilation.* Westport: Greenwood Press, 1986.

Wedemeyer, General Albert C. *Wedemeyer Reports!* New York: The Devlin-Adair Company, 1958.

Wegner, Bernd. *Hitlers Politische Soldaten: Die Waffen SS.* Paderborn: Ferdinand Schöningh, 1982.

Weidinger, Otto. *Division Das Reich.* 5 Vols. Osnabrück: Munin Verlag, 1967–1982.

Weinberg, Gerhard L. *A World at Arms.* New York: Cambridge University Press, 1994.

Weingartner, James. *Crossroads of Death.* Berkeley: University of California Press, 1979.

———. *Hitler's Guard.* Carbondale: Southern Illinois University Press, 1974.

Westphal, General Siegfried. *The German Army in the West.* London: Cassel, 1951.

Whaley, Barton. *Covert German Rearmament, 1919–1939: Deception and Misperception.* Frederick, Md.: University Publications of America, 1984.

Whiting, Charles. *Massacre at Malmedy.* London: Leo Cooper, 1971.

Williams, Maurice. "German Imperialism and Austria, 1938." *Journal of Contemporary History.* Vol. 14, No. 1, (January 1979): pp. 139–153.

Williamson, Gordon. *Infantry Aces of the Reich.* London: Arms and Armor Press, 1991.

Wilmot, Chester. *The Struggle For Europe.* New York: Harper and Brothers Publishers, 1952.

Wilson, John B. "Influences on U.S. Army Divisional Organization in the Twentieth Century." *Army History.* No. 39, (Fall 1996): pp. 1–7.

Winton, Harold R. *To Change an Army*. Lawrence: University Press of Kansas, 1988.

Zaloga, Steven J. "Technological Surprise and the Initial Period of War: The Case of the T-34 Tank in 1941." *The Journal of Slavic Military Studies*. Vol. 6, No. 4, (December 1993): pp. 634–646.

————, and Grandsen, James. *Soviet Tanks and Combat Vehicles of World War II*. London: Arms and Armor Press, 1984.

————, and Madej, Victor. *The Polish Campaign, 1939*. New York: Hippocrene Books, 1985.

Ziemke, Earl F. *Stalingrad to Berlin: The German Defeat in the East*. Washington, D.C.: U.S. Army, 1968.

————, and Bauer, Magna E. *Moscow to Stalingrad: Decision in the East*. Washington, D.C.: U.S. Army, 1987.

Zilbert, Edward R. *Albert Speer and the Nazi Ministry of Arms*. London: Associated University Presses, 1981.

Zwehl, General Hans von. "Gedanken eines britischen Offiziers uber den Zukunftskrieg." *Militär Wochenblatt*. Vol. 108, No. 6 (25 September 1923): pp. 128–129.

Index

Page numbers in italics indicate illustrations

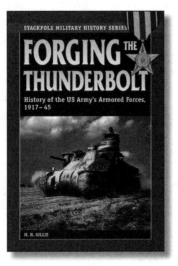

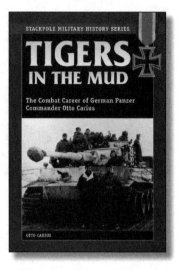

Stackpole Military History Series

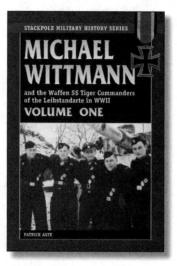

MICHAEL WITTMANN AND THE WAFFEN SS TIGER COMMANDERS OF THE LEIBSTANDARTE IN WORLD WAR II
VOLUME ONE
Patrick Agte

By far the most famous tank commander on any side in World War II, German Tiger ace Michael Wittmann destroyed 138 enemy tanks and 132 anti-tank guns in a career that embodies the panzer legend: meticulous in planning, lethal in execution, and always cool under fire. Most of those kills came in the snow and mud of the Eastern Front, where Wittmann and the Leibstandarte's armored company spent more than a year in 1943–44 battling the Soviets at places like Kharkov, Kursk, and the Cherkassy Pocket.

$19.95 • Paperback • 6 x 9 • 432 pages • 383 photos • 19 maps • 10 charts

WWW.STACKPOLEBOOKS.COM
1-800-732-3669

Stackpole Military History Series

MICHAEL WITTMANN AND THE WAFFEN SS TIGER COMMANDERS OF THE LEIBSTANDARTE IN WORLD WAR II
VOLUME TWO
Patrick Agte

Barely two months after leaving the Eastern Front,
Michael Wittmann and the Leibstandarte found themselves in
Normandy facing the Allied invasion in June 1944. A week after D-Day,
Wittmann achieved his greatest success, single-handedly destroying
more than a dozen British tanks and preventing an enemy
breakthrough near Villers Bocage. He was killed several months later
while leading a Tiger battalion against an Allied assault. The
Leibstandarte went on to fight at the Battle of the Bulge and in
Hungary and Austria before surrendering in May 1945.

$19.95 • Paperback • 6 x 9 • 400 pages • 287 photos • 15 maps • 7 charts